ENDORSEMENTS

The Small Wonders of Leadership is replete with examples of great historical leaders and their defining traits. Traits that many of today's leaders seem to be lacking. Everyone can improve their leadership skills, whether personal or professional, by adopting the principles in this book.

- Roger Miller
Owner, The Utah Jazz and the Larry H. Miller Group of Companies

The Small Wonders of Leadership is a great book on principle-based leadership that I would recommend to any business leader who wants to improve his or her effectiveness and impact on those around them. Too often, people advance in their careers and become managers because of individual achievement without being grounded in principles of leadership. This is a must read for all new leaders and managers and provides a benchmark in best practices for those more seasoned leaders. *The Small Wonders of Leadership* should be required reading at colleges and universities across all disciplines for all those who aspire to positions of leadership and influence.

- Daniel T. Burdick
Vice President, Goldman Sachs

James M. Morrison is rapidly emerging as a leader and effective teacher of valuable life lessons. Not only will leaders do well to read *The Small Wonders of Leadership*, but each of us as individuals should learn its concepts to be better people and positive contributors to society.

- Blair B. Asay
Presdient/CEO, Hi-Land Credit Union

As a sworn police officer for more than 15 years, I have seen the heartache and atrocities that could have been avoided if the principles of this book were incorporated into individual lives. Compassion and love would prevail. The cruelty I have witnessed because of selfishness would be replaced with charity. This book, The Small Wonders of Leadership, is full of wisdom yet the message that was most profound was true leaders, whether in the home, business or community must never be self-proclaimed, but must earn that role through honorable and loving actions, showing true concern for the worth of individuals.

It has been my privilege to know James Morrison, and I can confirm with the upmost confidence that the power of this book comes from an author that lives and practices the principles contained within. Take the time to read and ponder the words, then take action to make your life and those you come in contact with more fulfilling.

- John G. Freeman
Category 1 Peace (Police) Officer

The Small Wonders of Leadership makes you stop and think of where you can improve, what steps your going to take to implement, what a person could do to inspire complete team work, and how one can effectively communicate and rally those you interact with. The book, in its simple form of philosophy, creates a lifetime resource for internal change and external influence.

- Mark Runia
Owner, Finishline Express
Founder, Board of Directors, H2toGo

The world is asking for moral leadership. *The Small Wonders of Leadership* contains timeless principles for moral leaders and is an effective catalyst for change. It takes leadership to the highest level. This book is a must read for anyone in a leadership position.

- Karen Thomson
School Administrator

The Small Wonders of Leadership truly provided essential insight and reflection into concepts of leadership and principles of integrity. What's more, it gave me a desire to be better each day in every way. Each Chapter provided tremendous motivation and the thoughts shared throughout every paragraph enticed me to excel in every aspect of life. The book is anything but a small wonder, it's more like a major miracle maker.

- Randy Allen

Associate Chief Administrative Officer and Former Chief Financial Officer for Salt Lake County

The *SMALL WONDERS* of Leadership

THE PHILOSOPHY IS ITS POWER

James M. Morrison

Printed in the United States of America

Design by Andrew J. Siddoway
Chief Editor: Andrew J. Siddoway

The Small Wonders of Leadership: The Philosophy is It's Power
James M. Morrison - 1st ed.

ISBN: 978-0-9839434-1-9

10 9 8 7 6 5 4 3 2 1
First Edition

This book is dedicated to the thousands of men and women I have had the opportunity to work with, learn from, and to teach.

TABLE OF CONTENTS

No leadership position should be maintained unless by the conduct of appropriate behavior because of the influence it has on those being led.

James M. Morrison

The Small Wonders of Leadership
The Philosophy Is Its Power

Leader & Follower
- A symbiotic relationship -

Civility
- Society is built on sound principles -

Leading in Front
- If you are out of sight you are out of touch -

Self Control
- There is no excuse -

Accountability
- Justice and Mercy -

Attitude
- Authentic personal power -

Must Act
- Everything translates into hard work -

Vision
- The future must be created -

Enthusiasm & Optimism
- Mirror images of strength -

Master Communicator
- Influence people with honor -

No Man Is An Island
- A basic need to belong to a community -

PREFACE

In today's world of dilated and dramatized unrest and trouble, for which there seems to be no solution, leaders ought to pause and reflect on the influences and consider the remedies that will bring back stability and sanity. The essential thesis requires a cadre of trained and well-disciplined leaders. In calling for such specific goals as discipline, obedience, contagious enthusiasm, and other small wonders of leadership is nothing new in the annals of history.

The bond leaders tie between ethics and the leadership role provides the strength and authority to lead effectively. Of all the skills and concise studies of historical leadership, the skill of discipline and obedience must be among the most exacting. The end value of such standards and modes of behavior are the instruments of leadership capacity.

The concept of moral leadership concerns me the most. The dramatic emergence during the last decade of unethical leadership influencing followership is of the most serious failures of any enterprise. I contend there is significant and possibly volcanic destruction because of immoral and unbridled control in the responsibility and duty of a leader and those who choose to follow.

Employees of today are shouting from the mountaintops, bellowing from the valleys below echoing the need for the intangibles of loyalty, direction, enthusiasm, and all other indispensable quality traits of leadership. Despite the continued discussions and awareness around meeting the basic needs of employees, the problem continues to be chronic. If this were not the case, there would not be all the focused attention on the subject of moral leadership.

In spite of all the knowledge and training available, executing and practicing on the soft concepts continues to be elusive. In the broader discussion of leadership development, the fundamental tenets is simply meeting the basic human needs followed closely by the unremitting ability to execute on the importance of the organization's purpose.

Visualize the significance in the world if all present-day leaders embraced such concepts, which transcend time, culture, ethnicity, and space. This generation of the twenty-first century might be the era of the new leader.

LEADER & FOLLOWER

A Symbiotic Relationship

The ability for an individual to self manage produces the power to initiate the influence to lead others. It is the precipice by which the landscape of the followership meets the demand of the leader. Leadership of self is far more important than leadership of others. If the leader is to be a role model and support system, they must meet the long-standing patterns of humanity and moral ethics. From the most complex societies to the simplest forms of self, there must be moral behavior centered on a value system for a given purpose.

Many years ago, General Mark W. Clark said of leadership: "All nations seek it constantly because it is the key to greatness, sometimes to survival…the electric and elusive quality known as leadership. Where does juvenile delinquency begin? In leaderless families. Where do slums fester? In leaderless cities. Which armies falter? Which political parties fail? Poorly led ones. Contrary to the old saying that leaders are born not made, the art of leading can be taught and it can be mastered."

From the lectern of life, the speech for greater leadership in all the horizontal areas of life, from the home and schools to the communities and corporate boardrooms. The essence of the speech is people need to govern based on principles such as truth, respect, decency, direction, accountability, and law and order even when it is unpopular to do so.

Over the course of history, there has been steady development in societies and communities. The strength and growth of civilizations has been rooted in ethics to drive the behavior of the people. Regrettably, in the wide battlefront to maintain cohesive communities, the devastation and destruction turns largely on individuals who consider their own welfare more important than that of the society or concern for one another. Today, we see the destructive aftermath of countries like Iraq, Libya, Iran, and within organizations such as Enron, Fannie Mae, and Global Crossing. The failure centers on the abuse of leadership.

Mao Tse-tung said, "To link oneself with the masses, one must act in accordance with the needs and wishes of the masses….. There are two principles here: one is the actual needs of the masses rather than what we fancy they need, and the other is the wishes of the masses, who must make up their own minds instead of our making up their minds for them….We should pay close attention to the well-being of the masses, from the problems of land and labor to those of fuel, rice, cooking oil and salt….We should help them to proceed from these things to an understanding of the higher tasks which we have put forward….Such is the basic method of leadership."

Arguably, a leader who violates natural establishments of leadership and enslaves the followers, needs to transform their behavior to support the well-being of the community. Otherwise, the followers will choose to follow someone else; the relationship will be compromised. On the other hand, followers who disrupt and do not yield to the main needs of the leader, create obvious grievances. As stated in my earlier book, *The Choice of Leadership*, "The role of a leader is even more complex than in years past because of the nature between the leader and follower relationship. In dialogue of the effects and multiplicity of needs, the core competencies are the hallmark of leadership to rise above the approach of inconsistency and to respect the legitimacy to reconcile the relationship between leader and follower."

The catalyst that converts mediocre leaders and followers to great leaders and followers is to live in harmony to the set standards and the discipline to live the small wonders of leadership. This concept would appear to be a simple one, but in essence, it is the soft skills that ultimately crushes most leaders and followers ability to be effective.

The social and corporate background is in a downward spiral, which is creating havoc and destruction to those in close proximity to the one in charge. With such chaos, the leader who requires commitment, dedication, discipline, and perhaps selflessness from those he or she leads becomes lost. It becomes lethal, to all those who are trying to lead and follow, when there is destructive behavior and little to no self-control in the symbiotic relationship.

In the book, *Journal of the Discovery of the Source of the Nile*, John Hanning Speke recounts the story with King Mtesa of Uganda. "The king now loaded one of the carbines I had given him with his own hands, and giving it full-cock to a page, told him to go out and shoot a man in the outer court, which was no sooner accomplished than the little urchin returned to announce his success with a look of glee such as one would see in the face of a boy who had robbed a bird's nest, caught a trout, or done any other boyish trick. The king said to him, 'And did you do it well?' 'Oh, yes, capitally.'" There was no thought or concern for the man shot. There was no discussion as to who the man was and the implication of their decisions.

The question arises from the role of leader and follower: Where are the ethics to dictate behavior? Or, is it merely based on one's desires and motives? One of the immutable laws of life is the privilege of choice. However, agency does not suggest doing wrong or violating the rights and privileges of other people. Agency is the ability to make appropriate choices based on the difference of right and wrong. The nature of the law is that each law has a consequence. Many people believe that governance is onerous which limits freedom and growth. Consequently, the exact opposite is true. Those who keep the law have greater freedom as opposed to those who disobey. Stable and healthy communities flow from obedience to such laws. There are rules and guidelines that regulate any community whether it is an individual or society.

The patterns of healthy societies are to have obedience and not merely conformity. These terms are most useful when describing the difference in people. Obedience is to live by a set standard and not to carbon copy every individual in the community. Influential leaders do not ask their followers to be anything less than unique. The full measure of a person is in the distinct personalities and skill-sets from all others; leaders and followers are not all exactly the same, but they do obey the outlined standards of the group.

In the book, *Leadership*, James MacGregor Burns expresses the idea of conformity, "Conformity does not depend on equal status among the members of the group; usually group statuses are closely perceived, and this may make for greater conformity, depending on the internal structure of the group and its extra group relations. Members of groups usually rank one another informally on the basis of such factors as the recognized ability of the group member to relate to the group goals, the extent to which the person lives up to group norms and follows group-approved procedures, and personal qualities that have no special relevance to the group but are highly valued in culture."

Leaders have the responsibility to skillfully build a rock solid ethical foundation and to show it in daily action. Abraham Lincoln said, "A house divided against itself cannot stand... Our cause must be entrusted to, and conducted by its own undoubted friends—whose hands are free, whose hearts are in the work—who do care for the results." In the broadest meaning, the house of leadership and followership must stand together. Leadership has to meet the basic needs of the followership and followership has to support the needs and aspirations of leadership. Nowhere is there a leader without a follower and follower without a leader. In essence, it is the same person because the traits of a leader and a follower are exactly the same. Even though the person might look and feel the same, the roles are different.

Throughout history, there have been institutionalized directives or constitutions that serve as a vital part of government to guide ethical behavior. From the beginning of time, civilizations have presented codes of conduct—the code Hammurabi, the Ten Commandments of the Hebrew, and the Edicts of Emperor Ashoka. The ultimate flow of effectiveness is in pools of specific value systems. Outlined and established ethics pave the way for cultural discipline.

There is a church of San Pietro in Vincoli in Rome, which is best known as being the home of Michelangelo's statue of Moses. Moses was often referred to as a religious leader, lawgiver, and prophet. He lived between 1391-1271 BCE when the children of Israel were increasing in population. Moses is one of the first influential leaders and authoritative figures in history. He was a leader of the people and set standard and announced law and a value system. In the background of the political stage, the Children of Israel, in the absence of Moses, worshipped a golden calf. With the return of Moses with tablets in hand, he recognized Israel's higher needs and helped Israel realize their own direst necessities.

David McClelland says, "He cannot inspire his people unless he expressed vivid goals which in some sense they want. Of course, the more closely he meets their needs, the less 'persuasive' he has to be; but in no case does it make sense to speak as if his role is to force submission. Rather it is to strengthen and uplift, to make people feel that they are the origins, not the pawns, of the socio-political system." The leader carries the responsibilities to meet the needs and goals of the community. The role of leadership is a collective one for those who belong and acts for its best interests, which are similar to those of their own. Arthur Bentley wrote, "Leadership is not an affair of the individual. It is fundamentally an affair for the group."

Some 2,500 years ago a young prince, Siddhartha Gautama,

ventures in search of truth and a spiritual path. He leaves the distractions of life and ponders concepts at Deer Park of Sarnath. He learned leadership was a set of pragmatic laws for self and for the world. He became known as Buddha offering the teaching of Buddhadharma.

One of the most significant events in history is that of the Constitutional Convention held in Philadelphia to address the concerns of governing the United States of America. It had been operating under the Articles of Confederation following the independence from Great Britain. On September 17, 1787, thirty-nine of the fifty-five attendees signed the document.

We, the People of the United States, in order to form a more perfect Union, establish Justice, insure domestic Tranquility, provide for the common Defense, promote the general Welfare, and secure the Blessing of Liberty to ourselves and our prosperity, do ordain and establish this Constitution for the United States of America.

The equilibrium of liberty and rights rests on the structure of such governance as the United States Constitution. The effectiveness of any group turns on the set guidelines to align the vast differences, backgrounds, experiences, attitudes, and interests of each individual. The essential role of a leader is to institutionalize value systems, which act for the needs of both leader and follower. The process for leadership and followership is the requirement for discipline; leaders and followers must be dedicated to the process and its success rests on the instruction of ethics.

John Adams understood the premise of the role of governance when he wrote: "Suppose a nation in some distant region should take the Bible as their only law book and every member should regulate his conduct by the precepts there exhibited. Every member would be obligated in conscience to temperance and frugality and industry, to justice and kindness and charity toward his fellowmen, and to piety, love, and reverence toward Almighty God. In this commonwealth no man would impair his health with gluttony, drunkenness or lust. No man would sacrifice his precious time to cards or trifling with other mean amusements. No man would steal or lie or in any way defraud his neighbor, but would live in peace and goodwill toward all men. No man would blaspheme his Maker or profane his worship, but a rational and manly, a sincere and unaffected devotion would reign in the hearts of all men. What a utopia, what a paradise this region would be."

In the United States, as in any form of a group, leadership must embrace the dexterity to gather the wide support and qualities for a sustained, long-range, and purposeful movement behind set standards.

What are my LEADER character traits that would allow a person to be willing to follow me?

_____

_____

_____

_____

_____

_____

_____

_____

_____

_____

_____

_____

_____

_____

_____

_____

_____

_____

*The **Small Wonders** of Leadership*
Leader & Follower - A Symbiotic Relationship

What are my FOLLOWER character traits that would allow a leader to empower me?

_____

_____

_____

_____

_____

_____

_____

_____

_____

_____

_____

_____

_____

_____

_____

_____

_____

_____

_____

*The **Small Wonders** of Leadership*
Leader & Follower - A Symbiotic Relationship

How would others describe my strengths and weaknesses?

_____

_____

_____

_____

_____

_____

_____

_____

_____

_____

_____

_____

_____

_____

_____

_____

_____

_____

_____

_____

_____

*The **Small Wonders** of Leadership*
Leader & Follower - A Symbiotic Relationship

CIVILITY

Society Is Built On Sound Principles

As history recently closed the 20th century and opened the 21st century, the cultural aspect of the new century is taking on new shapes and many forms. The roots that laid deeply in a value system of civility, in the prior century, are now exposed causing harm and unprecedented destruction. At the beginning of the new century, people have adopted their own moral codes of conduct, which shapes the landscape of today. Those who are not guided by universal ethical principles such as kindness, compassion, and respect, create conflict, which permeates all relationships that contribute to the group or social ills.

Alfred Adler, highlights his theory of personality with the unique capacity of human beings to empathize in a much broader context of caring for family, for community, for society, and for humanity, even for life. The development of the individual and of the community enlists members to pursue common goals. Human nature is to belong and contribute to the group for a "community feeling" or "social interest".

From time-to-time, people can live happily in spite of others, but the true joy of life is found in good relationships. The key that unlocks all healthy relationships is civility. Everyone needs to learn how to live well with others.

Adam Smith, the author of *The Wealth of Nations* (1776), wrote an earlier book *The Theory of Moral Sentiments* (1759), which provides an ethical and philosophical underpinning wherein he laid out the foundational moral philosophy of civility by which a free market economy and a constitutional political society survives. The central theme is sympathy to identify with the emotions of others and maintain good relations with their fellow human beings. He taught the balance of benevolent acts and support for the general social order and upon the essential morality of the people. When those are gone, ultimately the free market economy and the constitutional political society will be compromised and will be destroyed. Dr. Kirk Hart writes, "The future of America seems problematic….These heightened times call for the highest qualities of civic character from both leaders and citizens."

Years ago, I remember watching on the news the lawlessness in Los Angeles during the trial for Rodney King's attackers. Thousands of people looted, assaulted, and many were murdered. Cars were being burned and storefront windows smashed; people were happily carrying out stolen goods. The social ills and moral decay was such that there appeared to be an underexposed teaching to civility.

President John F. Kennedy stated, at an American University commencement address in June 1963, "So, let us not be blind to our differences—but let us also direct our attention to our common interests and to means by which those differences can be resolved. And if we cannot end now our differences, at least we can help make the world safe for diversity. For, in the final analysis, our most basic common link is that we all inhabit this planet. We all breathe the same air. We all cherish our children's future. And we are all mortal."

Making contact with real truth creates a broadening and deepening base from which to behave. The Polar star is a visible star that is aligned less than a degree from the North Pole of the earth's axis of rotation. Through the centuries, travelers used the star's constant position to provide direction. At night, mariners fixed their sights on the North Star, which provided an anchor for safety to their destination.

Like the sky's guide to the travelers, people need to operate based on fixed principles and truths as opposed to the social dictates of the current environment. The transcending values of principles will provide the strength to remain morally civil.

Principles are truths that transcend time, space, ethnicity, age, gender, and furthermore, do not discriminate along any lines. All principles have predictable outcomes. Such principles of human conduct have the same characteristics as principles of science. Gravity applies everywhere in the world, it operates on people of different ethnicity, age, and social class. Principles do not look for approval in order to operate. Regardless of how one feels about the principle, it applies its immutable predictable outcomes when acted upon.

Take the example of a young man in China or an old woman across the world in the United States who simultaneously step off a tall building. The consequence is a fall to earth. Contrast the principles of science to the equally strong principles of human conduct. The striking example of respect when violated will produce the same negative result regardless of the person, time, or place. There will be hurt feelings and possible resentment.

When people fail to embrace principles of human conduct, the natural consequence will be destroyed relationships and inevitable division in social environments. There is the compelling argument to learn to transcend ourselves into the place of other people. Henry James once said, "Three things in human life are important: The first is to be kind. The second is to be kind. And the third is to be kind."

In the movie, *The Ten Commandments*, Moses tells the Pharaoh, "We are to be governed by God's law, not by you." The essence of his message implies: We will not be governed by others unless that person embodies the law. Natural principles and laws govern the most stable societies and organizations.

Individuals cannot supersede principles and natural laws; they cannot wear two faces and expect to have cohesive societies. They are not chameleons that change their hues to fit their self-serving advantages.

One of the most devastating events was the Amish school shooting at the West Nickel Mines School in Bart Township, Pennsylvania on October 2, 2006. A dairy truck driver walked into a one-room Amish schoolhouse killing four girls and wounding seven before killing himself. The fifth child died the next morning following the shooting. The gunmen held an apparent 20-year grudge against the community. "When Mr. Roberts arrived at the school shortly before 10:30 a.m., he was carrying a 9-millimeter handgun…when the state police arrived around 10:45, Mr. Roberts had barricaded the doors with bolts and lumber he had brought in his pickup truck."

"After a brief cell phone exchange with his wife and then with the state police, Mr. Roberts began shooting, aiming the handgun and a shotgun at the children as they stood lined in front of the room."

In an article, *Amish Say They 'Forgive' School Shooter*, "We arrived in this community of Nickel Mines, Pa., curious about how the Amish, who live differently than most Americans do, might react to what was an unthinkable act of violence. It didn't take long for us to learn that the Amish families most affected by this tragedy have responded in a way that might seem foreign to most of us: They talk about Monday's school shooting only in terms of forgiveness."

There was no scapegoat to become irrational and a victim to the social environment rather an opportunity to apply a principle of forgiveness. The story continues of an Amish mother showing up at the gunmen's home not to confront the widow of the murderer holding her responsible for the senseless act, but to visit the home because of her compassion for his kin who were also suffering from tremendous pain. The response was the start of healing as opposed to the deep seeded hatred that is often the road most traveled.

Everyone, not to the extent as in the small township of Bart, Pa., from time-to-time will experience the heavy weight of life. The pointed question: How does a person transition from the dictates of a victim mentality to the shaping values of the social fabric? The power flows from the elemental influence of principles and espoused values of the group. It is called civility. The entire structure becomes rooted in the common culture of the basic shared motives and goals of everyone.

Guy de Maupassant, the French writer, tells the story of a peasant named Hauchecome who came to the village on market day. While walking through the public square, his eye caught sight of a piece of string lying on the cobblestones. He picked it up and put it in his pocket. His actions were observed by the village harness maker, with whom he had previously had a dispute.

Later in the day the loss of a purse was reported. Hauchecome was arrested on the accusation of the harness maker. He was taken before the mayor, to whom he protested his innocence, showing the piece of string that he had picked up. But he was not believed and was laughed at.

The next day the purse was found, and Hauchecome was absolved of any wrongdoing. But, resentful of the indignity he had suffered because of a false accusation; he became embittered and would not let the matter die. Unwilling to forgive and forget, he thought and talked of little else. He neglected his farm. Everywhere he went, everyone he met had to be told of the injustice. By day and by night he brooded over it. Obsessed with his grievance, he became desperately ill and died. In the delirium of his death struggles, he repeatedly murmured, "A piece of string, a piece of string."

Like Hauchecome, many can repeat the story in their own lives unless there is a much stronger foundation built on the edifying principles to govern behavior. The words of Abraham Lincoln in his Second Inaugural Address helped to heal the wounds of the of the United States of America.

With Malice toward none; with charity for all; with firmness in the right as God gives us to see the right, let us strive on to finish the work we are in, to bind up the nation's wounds, to care for him who shall have bourne the battle and for his widow and his orphan, to do all which may achieve and cherish a just and lasting peace among ourselves, and with all nations.

The extent to which groups tie together all the civility to behave in accordance with the motives, needs, attitudes, and values, the more the group becomes a concrete, solid, and durable foundation in human society.

What are the key principles and values that sustain a civil community?

_____
_____
_____
_____
_____
_____
_____
_____
_____
_____
_____
_____
_____
_____
_____
_____
_____
_____
_____
_____

*The **Small Wonders** of Leadership*

Civility - Society Is Built On Sound Principles

What are the core principles and values I embrace?

_____

_____

_____

_____

_____

_____

_____

_____

_____

_____

_____

_____

_____

_____

_____

_____

_____

_____

_____

_____

_____

_____

_____

*The **Small Wonders** of Leadership*

Civility - Society Is Built On Sound Principles

How can I genuinely contribute to my community?

_____
_____
_____
_____
_____
_____
_____
_____
_____
_____
_____
_____
_____
_____
_____
_____

The **Small Wonders** _of Leadership_

Civility - Society Is Built On Sound Principles

LEADING IN FRONT

If You Are Out of Sight You Are Out of Touch

enturies ago, a leader's place was up-front in the most visible position leading the way into battle astride their horse or in front in a chariot. Influential leaders show the way and are never in the neutral place of the office. Alexander the Great and Caesar inspired, cheered, and encouraged their warriors against all odds. A great leader will always lead in front and never from the obscurity of behind.

Consider the classic story of Florence Nightingale. In the book by Lytton Strachey, *The Biography of Florence Nightingale* wrote of her, "For to those who watched her at work among the sick, moving day and night from bed to bed, with that unflinching courage, with the indefatigable vigilance, it seems as if the concentrated force of an undivided and unparalleled devotion could hardly suffice for that first portion of her task alone. Wherever in those vast wards suffering was at its worst and the need for help was greatest, there, as if by magic, was Miss Nightingale."

She dedicated her entire life for the relief of pain and suffering. Above all the pursuits of her goal, was her purpose to create better conditions from the deplorable sanitary conditions for the men fighting in the Crimean War. The warehouse of beds where the sick and suffering men laid stretched over four miles with little to no space between them.

With vigilant consideration into the trait of leading in front, followers must not only hear, but also see the leader taking charge and assuming responsibility. It is impossible to assess too highly the influence of the leader who pays the price to understand the needs, motivations, and expectations of the group. The latitude, in which leaders take advantage of the teaching moments to inspire lasting impressions, are those who actively seek out others, provide vision and direction, nurture relationships, supply encouragement, hope, and strength is the choice between devotion or abandonment.

This one behavior and skill will help transform a society from disintegration to sustainable healthy communities, which is the most decisive course of action. Leadership is essentially the responsibility of venturing out front, going first, blazing the trail, and standing in front with the audiences of thousands.

The fixed conviction of a leader to influence and lead is abundantly all around. Those who do well and not isolate themselves from the opportunities will have greater influence to show the way. When leading in front, whatever the current leadership sphere is, it will naturally grow and eventually create critical mass for sustained stability. There are many people who are waiting for such visible authority to be led.

The Marine Corp is one of the finest institutions in the world. The credo appropriately identifies the superb military structure as "The few. The proud." Those officers that are placed in front to lead bring about the troops to stand out and be the very best. This form of leadership is the model of correct leadership; it requires a certain degree of boldness. It is the responsibility to be out in front, going first addressing and tackling the hard issues while leading with honor.

To be an effective leader in today's environment, one must be bold and inspirational to help others see the environment and set standards. Over two hundred years ago, George Washington's First Inaugural address said, "It would be peculiarly improper to omit, in this first official act my fervent supplication to that Almighty Being, who rules over the universe, who presides in the councils of nations, and whose providential aids can supply every human defect, that His benediction may consecrate to the liberties and happiness of the people of the United States a government instituted by themselves for these essential purpose."

The task of leadership is to bring a consciousness of purpose of what the group represents; the people need to have a solid footing of what it stands for and organize around it. The essential strategy is to believe in yourself and those who choose to follow and the discipline to act on the motives, values, and goals. The most effective and consequential leader is the person who has major goals and objectives, which activate the people to the purpose. This will allow the leader to emerge and become a visible figure to sustain the interest of the group.

Many years ago, Charles H. Malik, then secretary general of the United Nations said,

> *"I respect all men, and it is from disrespect for none that I say there are no great leaders in the world today. In fact, greatness itself is laughed to scorn. You should not be great today—you should sink yourself into the herd, you should not be distinguished from the crowd, you should simply be one of the many. The commanding voice is lacking. The voice which speaks little, but which when it speaks, speaks with compelling moral authority--this kind of voice is not congenial to this age. The age flattens and levels down every distinction into drab uniformity. Respect for the high, the noble, the great, the rare, the specimen that appears once every hundred or every thousand years, is gone. Respect at all is gone! If you ask whom and what people do respect, the answer is literally nobody and nothing. This is simply an unrespecting age--it is the age of utter mediocrity. To become a leader today, even a mediocre leader, is a most uphill struggle. You are constantly and in every way and from every side*

pulled down. One wonders who of those living today will
be remembered a thousand years from now--the way we
remember with such profound respect Plato, and Aristo-
tle, and Christ, and Paul, and Augustine, and Aquinas."

In today's atmosphere, the call is for conscious effort to build strong noble leaders who understand the consequences and affects on society and to be vigilant in the face of adversity and rise up beyond mediocrity and above indifference. It requires a bold voice for what is right and honorable.

One of the most crucial fighting campaigns during World War II was fought on the small island of Okinawa. William Manchester fought as a young man on the battlefront where he became wounded and thousands of his comrades lost their lives. Years later he returned to the hell of the Shuri Line battle and walked over its once battle-scarred land. William wrote of his duty, "Men, I now knew, do not fight for flag or country, for the Marine Corps or glory or any other abstraction. They fight for one another. Any man in combat, who lacks comrades who will die for him, or for whom he is willing to die, is not a man at all. He is truly damned."

On the face of great leaders is the look of doing the hard things even in the steep climb to act in terms of certain values and purpose; it is the duty. The responsibility is to assume the position of ancient times by leading in front. Leaders show the way and the more enduring responsibility is to serve as the true example.

The process is not an easy one because the lens of the microscope is always in scrutiny of the one in charge. The book, *The Choice of Leadership,* states, "The sharp view of leadership is the required strict accountability of self and to the extent in which it will provide a stronger landscape to hold others accountable for their own behavior and performance. People tend to perform and behave at the standards set by their leader. If a leader is not behaving or performing appropriately; it will be virtually impossible to hold others accountable for their own vista of behavior." Socrates said, "Let him who would move the world, first move himself."

If a leader lacks integrity, in most cultures the leader does not survive. In such a statement, there must be the discipline to understand the role of leading in front. It will shape and alter the conditions of those who try to follow. Seemingly, if the role model is in direct competition to the purpose and ethical standards, followers will be encumbered to determine who the leader is and what the leader represents. The duplicity of the leader creates distortion through which the leader becomes unrecognizable. Such a misrepresentation places the collective interests of the group into individual interests forcing people to go their separate ways.

What can I do to be more visible to those I lead?

_____
_____
_____
_____
_____
_____
_____
_____
_____
_____
_____
_____
_____
_____
_____
_____
_____
_____
_____
_____

*The **Small Wonders** of Leadership*

Leading In Front - If You Are Out Of Sight
You Are Out Of Touch

How do I interact when dealing with people of different backgrounds, values, and experiences?

_____

_____

_____

_____

_____

_____

_____

_____

_____

_____

_____

_____

_____

_____

_____

_____

_____

How do I inspire others?

_____

_____

_____

_____

_____

_____

_____

_____

_____

_____

_____

_____

_____

_____

_____

_____

_____

_____

_____

The **Small Wonders** of Leadership
Leading In Front - If You Are Out Of Sight
You Are Out Of Touch

SELF CONTROL

There Is No Excuse

In a world of deteriorating behavior, there must be a pronounced effort for greater self-control. One of a leader's skills to advance civilization is discipline and without it civilizations would not exist. Human beings are battling the front of frequent urges to behave in improper actions. The urges are so powerful that the contradiction exists between instant gratification and purpose.

The central question that sharply affects choices is: What is the purpose of life or the purpose of the group? What are the things that matter most? What makes others and me happy? What is the contribution to society?

The most obvious solution to dysfunctional cultural norms is the discipline to develop self-mastery over choices and not falter to the social acceptance that everything else controls behavior. The most secure test of self-control is the subordination of urges to behave in accordance to purpose and the identification of the predictable consequences.

A thought leader years ago said, "Some become enslaved with compulsive habits or yield to appetites or to improper actions, and plead that they are helpless before their habits—that they are compelled, persuaded; that temptation was stronger than their will to resist. But we can choose…. We can break bad habits; we can acquire good habits; we can choose what we think by the sheer determination to do so."

Whether someone accepts the paramount consideration of

self-control or not, it is however, tied to the purpose of one's life. The force behind any life is purpose, which gives the power to resist the depths of selling out to poor choices. The very nature of poor choices narrow the character and corrodes the purpose. It is the vehicle to move beyond the roadblocks to carry individuals and societies to reach life's destination. Unfortunately, the long-standing chronic problems are dominating society. There are too many social ills because of the absence of control: alcoholism, violence, obesity, crime, sexual excesses, drug abuse, and all other roadblocks.

One of the common threads and perhaps the only common thread to the destruction of many societies is the lack of self-control. The principle of self-control brings to bear the importance of human effort to operate on a base of purpose. Society's decay is eroding and hastening at an exponential rate unlike any other time in history, whether it was the era of the Egyptian, Roman, or Renaissance, whatever the time period of history one thing will always remain constant, the critical skill of self-control.

Many have heard of or have personally lived such stories of taking the wrong bus. There was a man who had the intention of going to San Francisco but he arrived in San Diego. Upon arriving, he became annoyed that he found himself in a different city. In spite of his good intentions and in spite of his efforts, he was not in San Francisco but rather in San Diego. Many people find themselves in similar situations of life. They have goals and aspiration in life but never tend to arrive in achieving the goals. Not one person ever aspires to have a dysfunctional habit or addiction that consumes their life. They ended up in the wrong place because they took the bus marked indulgence.

The success of humanity is measured by the ability to act based on principle rather than the emotional and physical tides eroding self-control. One of life's most visible and consequential lessons is the gauge of self-mastery. C.S. Lewis, in his book, *Mere Christianity*, wrote, "A man who gives into temptation after five minutes simply does not know what it would have been like an hour later. That is why bad people, in a sense, know very little about badness. They have lived a sheltered life by always giving in."

The inevitable devastation of lost control offers hammer like blows to a social structure. It can and certainly will crush the structure of homes, communities, countries and virtually every other pillar of society where people live. A lack of control is growing vile; it reaches out in ways that destroys everyone who is in close proximity to the one who is deficient.

Arguably, there exists a point of no return for all bad habits, which will invariably consume every aspect of life. The Niagara River flows from Lake Erie into Lake Ontario; the river flows for thirty-six miles in which boaters have free will to boat on the river in any direction until the point of no return. Unfortunately, many are not aware of the impending danger until it is too late. The Niagara Falls will naturally impose its power on anyone who ventures too close and will draw him or her over the edge.

The extent of decision-making is in the structure of values sharply defined and deeply etched in the core of the person. The ability to act and do what is right is based on the principles aligned to one's life, which governs the decision-making process. Individuals must reflect on the circumstances and situations that form thoughts on how to act; broadly interpreted as the practical reasoning of moral responsibility and the ethical beliefs of "should", "right", "wrong", "good", and "bad." One behaves based on how they think and the espoused values of their life.

The question remains: What are the exact margins of ethical conduct? The issue of ethics might appear to be complex; however, it is quite simple. Within each individual, there is a consciousness of moral conduct knowing right from wrong. Beyond the social pressure dictating correctness, there lies an even greater compass at the core of human beings, a human endowment that provides awareness of the principle, "Opposition in All Things"—right and wrong. This immutable law governs every aspect ranging from science to human behavior. For example, the opposition of day and night, fast and slow, good and bad, and humility and arrogance. A person's chosen responses and behaviors create either internal liberty or captivity. There is not an option in overriding the law of opposition; therefore actions lead to the support of moral decay or to the sustaining power of ethical progression.

The concept of opposition in all things fertilizes the essential endowment of life to choose based on the absolute law of free agency. Every person has the freedom to choose his or her own course of action—one is "free to choose" and "free to act" for oneself resulting in a consequence. In the book, *The Choice of Leadership*, "Underlining one of the powerful principles is absolute truths—truth that is never changing and remaining constant. Truth transcends culture, time, environment, and circumstance regardless of what people think is appropriate or inappropriate. Consequences emerge from behavior that are predictable in nature. The simple observation is a cause and effect relationship between behavior and consequence." Appropriate choices (self-control) present positive outcomes as opposed to inappropriate choice (lost-control) that present poor consequences.

Given the moral erosion of society and the establishment of such basic fundamental truths of consciousness between right and wrong—the question remains: Is there any way to change the courses of the ethical and moral slide facing the world? The direct answer is yes. It is in the deep resolve to live life centered on ethical principles, truth, and the cause of one's life. It translates to the very nature of moral behavior. It starts with every individual having a character planted in the landscape and the responsibility to garden the appropriate chosen behavior.

The important decision is the choice between the various activities based on need and purpose of the individual or group. The cause has a profound influence on the decision-making process. In absence of the cause or purpose, people are left to themselves without an internal compass to direct choices. Individual choices, which are made with less meaning and little to no significant value, need to subordinate the reactive urge for the strength of purpose. Arguably, people need to forego good things in order to choose the best thing. The yielding to the enticing of those things, which are good or better in place of best, may cost everyone involved.

As long as the contradiction exists between the various decisions, even though a particular choice is more costly, the choice of best has greater value. The right choice is not only making the choice rather it has everything to do with knowing what to do, how to do it, when to do it, in the correct way and all for the right reasons.

As people charter through the waters of life, it is apparent that everyone has their own oars of urge and temptation. Many have their weaknesses for creamy chocolate or any type of desert while other vices challenge others. Unfortunately, and sadly enough people who are bright and very capable and who simply know better fall to the temptation, destroying not only themselves but also those in close proximity and the extended social environment.

Sterling W. Sill wrote, "Sometimes we allow our minds or spirits to be taken prisoner without knowing the cause. We often hear someone say, 'Why did I ever do such a thing?' or 'What makes me as I am?' All people are free to decide whether or not they will become degenerate, but none are free afterward. The prison walls that we build against ourselves are very strong, and escape from them becomes very difficult." Looking forward toward freedom from the consequences of lost restraint is the vista of self-control over urges and temptations. There is nothing more essential, there is nothing more significant, there is nothing so important and ennobling than the self-control of one's choices.

What are the situations that traditionally provoke my poor behavior ?

_____
_____
_____
_____
_____
_____
_____
_____
_____
_____
_____
_____
_____
_____
_____
_____
_____
_____

**What is my immediate reaction when
I hear negative news?**

_____
_____
_____
_____
_____
_____
_____
_____
_____
_____
_____
_____
_____
_____
_____
_____
_____
_____
_____

The **Small Wonders** of Leadership
Self Control - There Is No Excuse

How can I demonstrate greater self-control?

_____
_____
_____
_____
_____
_____
_____
_____
_____
_____
_____
_____
_____
_____
_____
_____
_____
_____

*The **Small Wonders** of Leadership*
Self Control - There Is No Excuse

ACCOUNTABILITY

Justice And Mercy

The footing for a solid society is the virtues of Justice and Mercy. Arguably, these virtues appear to be in direct competition with one another. However, the exact opposite is true. One cannot have mercy without the exercise of justice. Mercy tempers the enforcement of justice when laws are broken to provide hope and correction. Such laws are given to provide conditions for healthy and safe environments for the people to live.

The most outwardly disciplined societies identify with the principle of accountability. The extent to which group leaders hold others accountable by applying justice rather than merely relying solely on mercy, converts poor behavior into cultivated virtues for harmonious cultures. Mercy cannot supersede justice but the leader can balance justice with mercy. Leaders cannot supersede laws and principles. The effects of laws and principles do not diminish the leader's purpose to care for those he/she leads.

Laws are given for the government of any social group and must be supported and endorsed to create the stability and control of those within the group and without. The essence of leadership is the extent to which they can support and live up to the standards and satisfy the needs of others and of the community. The leader's role is to bring the followers into the governing process for the achievement of purpose; it is the thrust for people to take flight for successful lives.

One of the foundational truths of life is that it is not a world of chance. Take the examples of the early dawn and the sun rising from the eastern skies. People do not go to bed wondering if the sun will rise from the western hemisphere let alone rising at all. When it rains, people are not encumbered to wonder whether the water will run up or down hill or the boiling and freezing points of 212 and 32 degrees Fahrenheit. The farmer who plants a seed is not questioning what crop will be harvested at the end of the season. In an orderly world, laws and principles produce predictable consequences in advance.

There are many forms of laws; legislative laws are traditionally arbitrary and regulatory enforced by some sort of a judicial system to control people. Such laws are just or unjust, right or wrong, and practical or impractical. The subjective laws are passed based on the current conditions of the environment to apply the necessary power of enforcement. They may be appealed or compromised in the same way through legislative enactment. Another form of law governs the universe to maintain order. Natural laws place order through the universal system.

Gravity remains constant and unalterable under all circumstances. There is no such influence to adjust or change the application of the principle. Man did not make them nor can man change them. The law of the farm is another natural law; there is complete order. The preparation, planting, and harvesting must all take place in its appropriate season. There is a time and season; planting does not happen in the winter when the ground is hard and cold and harvesting does not happen until after the planting and growth. If the farmer wants to be successful, he or she needs to learn how to follow the natural laws and live in harmony with them.

In order for people and any social structure to be successful, there must be a recognition and understanding of the power of governing laws and principles. A farmer who violates such laws will never reap the harvest. Wisdom and alignment to laws will predict outcomes in advance.

Such laws, as those of nature, there are other laws of human conduct, which operate under the same properties that of natural laws. They have their own properties of predictability and prophecy to cause or prevent specific events. Human laws transcend every fabric of life: time, space, ethnicity, culture, and demographic. They simply do not discriminate; the verdict is always the same and they apply to everyone: respect, kindness, accountability, compassion, direction and a list of many others. Understanding the human laws will regulate human behavior to produce better results.

As leaders reach out, the fingertip sensitivity is how to apply the human law of justice and mercy. When there is no accountability, the predictable consequence is everything spirals out of control. One of the most difficult things for most people is to judge behavior. Applying accountability of justice does not mean turning the back to those who fail to live up to the set standards rather an obligation to support and correct the erring person for greater discipline and obedience.

Leaders accompany justice with strength, courage, and the capacity to assist those in need. There is no benefit in ignoring the responsibility to allow deficiencies to wash over or around the leader. Effective leadership is based on those who respond to a code of ethics within the appropriate context of what is right or wrong.

One of the great cities was no other than the city of Athens. In its favorable conditions, it served as the central government, learning, science, and arts center. When the young men turned the age of 18 they each took an oath:

We will never bring disgrace on this our City by an act of dishonesty or cowardice.

We will fight for the ideals and sacred things of the City, both alone and with many.

We will revere and obey the City's laws, and will do our best to incite a like reverence and respect in those above us who are prone to annul them or set them at naught.

We will strive increasingly to quicken the public sense of civic duty.

Thus in all these ways we will transmit this City, not lessened, but greater and more beautiful than it was transmitted to us.

The demands of accountability for laws broken can be satisfied through mercy by greater conforming and continual obedience to the set standards which are absolutely central for a state of equilibrium.

The ultimate test of leadership is the balance between justice and mercy. One of the most devastating events ever to be played on the stage of American soil was the Civil War. It was a costly war in the amount of lives lost on the battlefield, and indescribable suffering throughout the entire social theater. The greatest scene performed was on April 9, 1865 at Appomattox, Virginia when General Robert E. Lee surrendered to General Ulysses S. Grant. General Grant delivered the terms and conditions under which the Confederate soldiers were free to return to their homes with their personal arms, their private horses, and baggage. There was no long speech of reparation, recrimination, or demands for punishment. The power of justice is fair but the power of mercy is far beyond fair. Despite all the difference and devastation to this country, the indispensable tool to heal the nation was the magnificent act of mercy.

The principles of justice and mercy must be tied together to create balance in the accountability process. The dynamic interaction between the principle of justice and mercy are the forces for momentum in the dominant leadership components. St. Thomas said, "Justice without Mercy is cruelty." It is a symbiotic relationship in which they deeply permeate each other. The relationship is the continued purpose of the individual and group. The good sense of rule motivates others to respect the hallmark standards for discipline. Unless others can see the full weight of leaders holding individuals accountable, the end result will be a weakened position to hold others responsible. What followers must see is a commanding figure who stands on a platform of principle and government to rise above the plateau of mediocrity.

Neal A. Maxwell, an educator said, "The leader who is willing to say things that are hard to bear, but which are true and which need to be said is the leader who truly loves his people and who is kind to them. Nothing is more cruel than that leader who in order to have the praises and plaudits of his followers entice them from safety into the swamp out of which some may never return."

Holding others accountable to the set standards brings about the conversion to help others align to set values, beliefs, and goals. On the other hand, the main source of conflict is the lack of accountability of the members of the group, which only enables dysfunction. From the leadership lectern is the speech of the governing principles to steward, guide, and mentor those who are willing to listen to the one in charge.

C.S. Lewis, in his book, *God in the dock: Essay on Theology and Ethic*, wrote, "The humanitarian theory wants simply to abolish Justice and substitute Mercy for it…Mercy, detached from Justice grows unmerciful." Society tends to lose the balance between the center point of justice and mercy by a rush to mercy instead of an appropriate charge of justice balanced with mercy. The counterbalance against justice is the thought to protect the individual from disappointment and hurt feelings even when the appropriate action to correct is necessary; this is unmerciful.

The essential aspect for everyone is to bring about the transformation by applying judgment in a merciful way. If all people, either the leader or follower can learn how to apply justice and mercy evenly, these virtues alone will give the power to create successful environments.

What are my feelings about being held accountable?

**What are the circumstances where I should
have received greater mercy?**

_____
_____
_____
_____
_____
_____
_____
_____
_____
_____
_____
_____
_____
_____
_____
_____
_____
_____
_____

What are the circumstances where I should have received greater accountability (justice)?

_____
_____
_____
_____
_____
_____
_____
_____
_____
_____
_____
_____
_____
_____
_____
_____
_____
_____
_____
_____

*The **Small Wonders** of Leadership*
Accountability - Justice And Mercy

ATTITUDE

Authentic Personal Power

Some of the greatest power rests within ourselves. However, the key to unlock the power is the fundamental law in which it rests. The atmosphere in which the law operates must never be taken for granted or overlooked. As people learn the principle, the climate to bring about a positive social environment will produce the joy of life. William James, the great Harvard psychologist said, "The greatest discovery of my generation is that human beings can alter their lives by altering their attitudes of mind."

Years ago, an associate shared this story: While a woman was waiting for her plane at London's Heathrow Airport, she purchased a package of English shortbread cookies. Making her way to a seating area, she carefully arranged her luggage and was getting settled when a man approached and indicated by pleasant gesture that he would like to occupy the seat next to her. She nodded and he sat down.

After a few minutes, the woman decided to eat some of the cookies she had purchased, and she reached down to get them. As she opened the package, she noticed the man beside her watching with great interest. She took the first cookie and began to eat when, to her great surprise, the man reached over, smiling and took the second cookie.

The women ate her cookie in stunned silence, astonished at the audacity of the man. After a moment, she determinedly reached for the third cookie, but no sooner had she taken it out of the package than he, again smiling and without a word, reached over and took the fourth. Her indignation rose as back and forth they went in total silence, she taking a cookie, he taking a cookie, until they reached the bottom of the package where the final cookie remained.

Without hesitation, the man reached over and took it, broke it in half, and cheerfully handed her one of the pieces. The women took her half of the cookie with an icy glare. After finishing his half, the man stood, still smiling. With a polite bow, he turned and walked away.

The woman could not believe that anyone could be so arrogant and rude. She was extremely flustered, her stomach churning. Making her way back to the airport gift shop, she picked up a package of antacid. As she opened her purse to get the money to pay for it, she stopped short. There in the bag was her unopened package of shortbread cookies!

From time to time, many have had the experience of becoming reactive to the environment rather than operating based on the strength of purpose. "Unfortunately, many individuals choose their attitudes based on their circumstances and situations—the social climate, rather than choosing their attitudes based on values. One who behaves from a profound sense of purpose can remain consistent regardless of the external environment of how others interact with them, social culture, and circumstance."

"The vital power of people is they are not a product of their environment, genetics, and psyche; rather they stand alone and independent from such settings. They have the ability to choose. In truth, there are countless opportunities to spring up to great heights and experience the full chambers of life. The utmost influence of a leader is the power of choice. They can choose their relationships, their friends, their careers, their behaviors and their emotions. The power is derived from intelligence to act for himself or herself as opposed to being acted upon as an inanimate object or some other animal or plant organism."

The truth of attitude is taken so lightly that it barely scratches the surface of many leadership discussions. In all parts of the world from New York to Beijing and from London to the United States, there are the results of destroyed relationships, families, and civilizations. People are setting aside the most influential resource they individually own for success and happiness. One of the most underdeveloped traits and greatest unused powers is attitude. Ultimately, everything can be taken from man except the freedom to choose his own attitude.

Dr. Russell H. Conwell was a Union officer in the Civil War and later became the founder of Temple University in Philadelphia. Beyond the great accomplishments of his life was the famous lecture entitled "Acres of Diamonds." It has been said Dr. Conwell had delivered the speech over 200 times a year over 25 years. The total admissions were over $4,000,000. The theme of the talk centered on an ancient Persian farmer by the name Ali Hafed who was very wealthy.

One day Ali Hafed had a visit from a Buddhist priest who was one of the best informed men of his time. That evening the priest sat before the fire with Ali Hafed and told him about the world and how it was made. He explained that the most valuable thing in the world was a diamond. The priest explained that a diamond was a drop of congealed sunlight. It was a deposit of carbon from the sun. The old priest told Ali Hafed that if he had one diamond the size of his thumb, he could purchase the entire community in which he lived. And if he could find a diamond mine, he could place his children upon thrones.

After Ali Hafed had learned about the diamond, he thought of nothing else and that night he went to bed a poor man. He had lost nothing, but he was poor because he now thought of himself as being poor. He now wanted diamonds more than anything else in the world. He lay awake all night thinking about these precious gems and how he could get them.

He inquired where diamonds might be found. The old priest did not know, but he told Ali Hafed that in some places in the world there were plenty of diamonds and all that anyone had to do was to find them. Ali Hafed made up his mind. He sold his farm, left his neighbor in charge of his family, took his money, and started out to search the world for diamonds.

He began his explorations at the mountains of the moon. Afterward he traveled throughout Asia. He searched in Palestine. He went to Europe. After years of searching his money had all been spent and he found himself in rage, wretchedness, and poverty. Then one day he stood on the shores of the bay of Barcelonia in Spain as a great tidal wave came rolling in between the pillars of Hercules. Then poor, afflicted, suffering Ali Hafed fell victim to the awful temptation to cast himself into the incoming tide. He sank beneath its foaming crest, never to rise again.

Back home the man who had purchased Ali Hafed's farm was one day letting his camel drink from the garden brook. As the camel splashed its nose into the shallow water of the clear stream, Ali Hafed's successor noted a curious flash of light coming from the white sands of the stream. He pulled out a stone that had an eye of light reflecting all the hues of the rainbow. He took the stone into his house and laid it on the mantel. Some time later when the same old priest came to visit Ali Hafed's successor he saw the light flashing from the mantel and told the owner that this stone was a diamond. Then together they rushed out into the garden and stirred up the white sands with their fingers, and lo, there came up other beautiful gems even more valuable than the first. Every part of that old farm produced valuable gems, which have since decorated the crowns of the greatest monarchs of the world.

This story has been shared as a historical account of the finding of the greatest diamond mine in the world, the Golconda diamond mine. The brilliant diamonds, Kohinoor and the Orloff of the crown jewels of England and Russia came from the farm of Ali Hafed. While Ali was exploring for the diamond mines of the world, he was living on the largest mine ever. The most powerful influence to any person is the power to choose one's attitude. There is no animal or thing that is endowed with the endless possibilities than the nature of man to own his or her attitude.

The story of Napoleon when he mentioned to England and Austria that he would move his massive army of 60,000 men with all of its artillery of tons of cannonballs and baggage up and over the Alps for battle illustrates the power of attitude. Unfortunately, to the demise of England and Austria they laughed at him because their attitude of the Alps was an impenetrable barrier that no one could cross. When Napoleon's engineers said, "Within the limits of possibility" Napoleon gave the command to go forward. He thought of himself to be a child of destiny. That is how one must think.

In order to achieve the future, one must improve the present and before any individual can improve the present, they must first improve their attitude. It is the dominant character trait to grow and achieve the possibilities of life. People's minds can certainly grow and expand, along with the other small wonders of leadership to move from the contracting positions of life to the stretching opportunities to achieve full ambition.

How would people describe my attitude?

_____
_____
_____
_____
_____
_____
_____
_____
_____
_____
_____
_____
_____
_____
_____
_____
_____
_____
_____
_____

The **Small Wonders** of Leadership

Attitude - Authentic Personal Power

How do I describe my attitude?

_____

_____

_____

_____

_____

_____

_____

_____

_____

_____

_____

_____

_____

_____

_____

_____

_____

_____

_____

_____

_____

*The **Small Wonders** of Leadership*
Attitude - Authentic Personal Power

What circumstances incite negative attitude?

_____

_____

_____

_____

_____

_____

_____

_____

_____

_____

_____

_____

_____

_____

_____

_____

_____

_____

*The **Small Wonders** of Leadership*
Attitude - Authentic Personal Power

MUST ACT

Everything Translates Into Hard Work

The most visible and consequential principle for any group to exist is the necessary requirement to act. No group or social order can maintain order or freedom without the enormously expanding skill of "Must Act". All members of the group must uphold the respective law of hard work for the protection and sustainable purpose of the assembly. Some 2,700 years ago, a Greek poet observed that "in front of excellence the immortal gods have put sweat, and long and steep is the way to it." Work is the essential resource guarding the group.

One of the immutable laws of nature is the principle of "The Law of the Harvest" as discussed in the chapter "Justice and Mercy." It is the law of sowing and reaping. If there is going to be a harvest, there will need to be a season of planting. The cycle of events and appreciation of the principle ranges along a continuum of preparation and hard work. True success is simply applied to natural laws; the law is applied across a vast range of functions from farmers to leaders of an organization.

Consider the nature and order of the process to bring a crop to market. The farmer is subject to governing laws of the farm. The farmer passes through a sequence of preparing the soil, planting the seed, protecting the crop to the extent possible from the harsh conditions of the environment and insects, nurturing with consistent water, weeding, harvesting, and lastly, selling.

The long and established practice of the farmer fertilizing the condition of the harvest with hard work, persistence, and follow through. From the beginning of time, there have been governing laws set in motion that naturally produce the results when lived in harmony to the laws. The obedience to such laws will produce the reward. The old proverbial saying, " What you sow is what you reap." The obvious fact that planting a grass seed produces grass, planting an apple seed produces an apple tree, planting an acorn does not produce an orange tree. It has been long recognized that laws have been put in place to govern actions and elements. People depend upon such laws and ethics for stability. The right seed needs to be planted to produce the right result.

Oprah Winfrey said, "The big secret in life is that there is no big secret. Whatever your goal, you can get there if you're willing to work."

Major Martin Treptow was killed in the battle of Chateau-Thierry in 1918. In the diary that was found on his body were written these words: "I will work; I will save; I will sacrifice; I will endure. I will fight cheerfully and do my utmost as though the entire conflict depended upon me alone." People must decide who and what they are to become. In fact, one point at which all men are measured is through determination. This might be the hardest job, which makes or breaks the success of the person.

Paradoxically, in the exercise of producing results, people sow one thing in hopes of reaping something entirely different; they attempt to decode the law and cheat the system. An obvious fact and one that is often forgotten is the calculated and conscious effort to short the system, which is in direct proportion to the result. The extent of the result varies directly with the stimuli to produce outcomes. Over the course of history, many individuals have aspired to accomplish lofty goals such as learning an instrument. If one only practices a minimal amount of time, the result is at best mediocrity. Arguably, when time has expired to develop, the tendency is to cram. How absurd it is to cheat the law of the harvest by preparing the soil, planting the seed, and harvesting crop all in the same season. The law of the harvest governs and people do not.

The human trait of hard work will produce the successes of life. With such consciousness of the potential, the explicit view will be an abundance of opportunity for the finer points of purpose. To the individual and the group, it is the centrality of continued existence and survival.

In the fourteenth century, Tamerlane and his army crossed Eurasia from Delhi to Moscow, from the Tien Shan Mountains of Central Asia to the Taurus Mountains in Anatolia; he swept across Asia and Europe. He conquered more than any other warrior except for Alexander. In the contemporary story, he never rested neither at the excuses of weakness or the increasing infirmities that could slow his formidable goals. In his early rise to building his empire, he suffered defeat at the hands of his enemy. In a desperate attempt to escape, he took refuge in a deserted ruin while the enemy searched for him.

While in solitary, he learned the theory that characterizes the principle of "must act" and perseverance. He noticed an ant carrying a kernel of corn, which was much larger and heavier than itself. Tamerlane saw the ant tugging and pushing the single grain up and over the wall. He watched the unavailing effort sixty-nine times to carry the corn up and over. Repeatedly, the heavy weight proved to be too much and the ant fell back with its burden, unable to prevail. Undeterred, the ant worked harder with deeper resolve to carry the grain over the wall. The seventieth time the ant carried away the grain in triumph. Tamerlane observed the ant's energy, ambition, drive, and courage, which was the source from which his own attitude altered to conquer armies.

The collectivity and varying degrees among the group to act is bound in the noble qualities of hard work and perseverance. Some of life's greatest people have been formed out of the concrete principles to rise above weakness. Ludwig von Beethoven was deaf when he finished some of the greatest musical compositions; John Milton was blind when he wrote *Paradise Lost;* Helen Keller was the first deafblind person to earn a Bachelor of Arts degree all of which left a permanent mark on the world.

Throughout the relatively brief history of the United States, one of the paramount legacies was that of Abraham Lincoln. "He was not born a king of men…but a child of the common people, who made himself a great persuader, therefore a leader, by dint of firm resolve, patient effort, and dogged perseverance. He slowly won his way to eminence and fame by doing work that lay next to him—doing it with all his growing might—doing it as well as he could and learned by his failure, when failure was encountered, how to do it better…. He was open to all impressions and influences, and gladly profited by the teaching of events and circumstances, no matter how adverse or unwelcome. There was probably no year of his life when he was not a wiser, cooler, and better man than he had been the year preceding."

Few things in life compare to the quality of hard work. The value of hard work builds character and helps improve society. Without hard work, there would be no scientists, doctors, teachers, or any advancement in science, medicine, or education. Work has been a central responsibility of the human experience from the beginning of time. No matter what the nature of the work is today, though likely different from that of Abraham Lincoln, the essential part of human condition is growth and development, which comes by hard work, diligence, commitment, and tenacity. The gift of hard work enhances life and self-reliance.

Over 2,000 years ago, an important event took place when Caesar took the front of his armies and led them across the Rubicon River. Today the phrase, "crossing the Rubicon" has been used to indicate the idea of "Must Act." In some sort of way, Caesar has become a role model for decisive action. Caesar knew the concise consequences when he entered the Northern part of Italy, where the river was the territorial boundary line. He knew what would happen if he attempted and failed. There must have been obvious hesitation before making the decision. When the decision was made, he would march to Rome with nothing wavering. Caesar said, "The die is cast." That expression embodies the time that deliberation had ended and the time was for action. There was no energies, strength, dedication, and focus that was left behind that would have deterred the success of the goal.

The first job of any person is the decision to work hard. Consciously or unconsciously every one is dependent on effort for accomplishment. However, there are innumerable examples of people who do the exact opposite. In the worldwide ideology, is the biased belief that life should be easy and the rewards should be immediate. The modern world emphasizes ease and instantaneous rewards. Although a society without work might seem attractive at first glance, without work a society will degenerate. There needs to be an awakening to the principle of "Must Act". Societies need to be stirred up and disrupted from their slumbering beds that provide comfort and complacency.

Life begins every morning and it becomes industrious when people become productive. Aristotle recited to Alexander the Great an important lesson about the close proximity of the enemy. He said, "The greatest enemy that ever confronts an army is never in the ranks of the foe, but always in your camp." What everybody must know is that individuals cannot expect others to do the hard work and reap the rewards. The biggest enemy to any person is their own lack of effort to produce the results for success. It is difficult to protect people from themselves.

Lofty goals and ambitious purpose give greater physical, spiritual, mental, and emotional strength to work honorably. The power to have meaningful lives lies within every individual. However, most people are in the exact situation because they are deliberately throwing the joys of life and everything that goes with it out in the garbage because they choose not to work.

How do I view work?

The **Small Wonders** of Leadership
Must Act - Everything Translates Into Hard Work

How do other people view my work ethic?

The **Small Wonders** of Leadership
Must Act - Everything Translates Into Hard Work

Identify the characteristics of hard work?

_____

_____

_____

_____

_____

_____

_____

_____

_____

_____

_____

_____

_____

_____

_____

_____

_____

_____

_____

*The **Small Wonders** of Leadership*

Must Act - Everything Translates Into Hard Work

VISION

The Future Must Be Created

In the broader discussion of the attributes to govern and one of the most fundamental tenets to effective leadership, is simply vision. This is the basic fundamental principle upon which other principles rest. This principle cannot merely wash over or around the narrow boundaries of the responsibilities of the leader. It is firmly linked to the understanding of human needs. There is no middle course between meaningless and significance; it is the signatory responsibility. The immediate needs of all people and groups is the purpose of existence and direction.

Vision translates into a base reality of meaningful purpose and contribution, which bind people together and inspire work ethic. The specific goal is to touch the individual's inner desires that benefit everyone who participates. It is the tip of the spear that pierces the hearts and minds to motivate and aspire for high achievement.

Throughout time, individuals gave their lives for their vision and subordinated life to the purpose and cause, to the extent in which it represented their life. In all the pages of the annals of history, the best index of leadership is the one that references vision. There are numerous stories that express the power of vision, Joan of Arc, a young warrior in battle, Martin Luther King, liberating people for equality, and John F. Kennedy, advancing space exploration. The pages continue to turn. The sharp affect of vision is the power and strength it provides to the group. The more active the vision the greater sense of commitment to belong to something much greater than self.

The story of 300 Spartans who fortified the pass of Thermopylae to keep the Persians from conquering Greece illustrates the nature of both the array of vision and will power. King Leonidas of Sparta led the small army in 480 BC of 300, which did not flee or surrender to the Persian army of hundreds of thousands. The Greeks held off the unlimited Persians soldiers for seven days until the rear-guard was annihilated in one of histories greatest last stand. Steven Pressfield, *Gates of Fire: An Epic Novel of The Battle of Thermopylae* wrote,

> *What kind of men were these Spartans, who in three days had slain before His Majesty's eyes no fewer than twenty thousand of His most valiant warrior? Who were these foeman, who had taken with them to the house of the dead ten, or as some reports said, as many as twenty for every one of their own fallen? What were they like as men? Whom did they love? What made them laugh? His Majesty knew they feared death, as all men. By what philosophy did their minds embrace it? Most to the point, His Majesty said, He wished to acquire a sense of the individuals themselves, the real flesh-and-blood men whom He had observed from the battlefield, but only indistinctly, from a distance, as indistinguishable identities concealed within the blood-and gore-begrimed carapaces of their helmets and armor.*

In the book, *The Choice of Leadership*, it says, "When everything seems vulnerable and ominous, even at the hands of the most extenuating circumstances and challenges, it is vision that keeps the human and organizational spirit alive to bear the adversities. Vision needs to lie within the fabric of every individual. It is what provides the strength to overcome the most unseemingly possibilities."

Vision produces the energy and the commitment to drive and pull people in a common direction. The power is in the ability to unify the masses with one voice and one purpose. Consequently, it resonates with all the people and allows them to be a part of something much larger than themselves; it provides purpose and meaning for their contribution. Vision is the formidable opportunity to do a very special and unique thing to unleash the human capital to accomplish what might ostensibly appear impossible to accomplish.

On May 25, 1961, John F. Kennedy announced before a special joint session of Congress the dramatic and ambitious direction of sending an American safely to the moon before the end of the decade. His purpose was to catch up and overtake the Soviet Union in the "space race". This was on the heels of Russia sending cosmonaut Yuri Gagarin who became the first human in space on April 12, 1961. NASA's program of human flight was guided by John F. Kennedy's vision. His goals were achieved on July 20, 1969, when Neil Armstrong uttered the extraordinary words, "One small step for man and one large step for mankind."

Of interest, the ultimate goal of putting a man on the moon was successfully accomplished six years after the death of the creator's vision. The thirty-fifth President of the United States, John F. Kennedy, was assassinated on Friday, November 22, 1963, in Dallas, Texas at 12:30 p.m.

John F. Kennedy's brief presidency reflects the staying power of vision and the importance of communicating the message to build a common purpose and set standards of excellence. The purpose unified the masses of people to execute on the most important goals and distinctive contribution of the organization. Vision can be so powerful that even opponents and naysayers cannot thwart the strength of the motivational effect of the few— exponential energy and motivation unleashes the esprit de corp.

John F. Kennedy's vision generated the commitment for the

nation to share in the importance of the ideals of the United States. In his inaugural address on January 20, 1961, he said, "Let every nation know, whether it wishes us well or ill, that we shall pay any price, bear any burden, meet any hardship, support any friend, oppose any foe, in order to assure the survival and the success of liberty."

Like lightening flashes in the night, the vision illuminated ambitious and noble commitment, which created synergy among all those involved. What seemed only plausible or even impossible became reality. An inspiring vision has made it commonplace for man's exploration in outer space. Space shuttles are launched so regularly into space that it hardly makes the news. The expressed vision to congress on May 25, 1961, not only satisfied the man on the moon, but also shattered the impossibilities of satellite transmission of billions of pieces of information. John F. Kennedy's vision paved the path for exponential growth in many industries including communications through cell phones, internet, and space exploration with space stations and galaxy discovery. It has utterly changed how people live.

In the late 1420's, a visionary figure emerged who became known as Joan of Arc. "The birth of Joan of Arc in a poor peasant home, her insistence on confronting military men who had little time for peasants, and much less for an eighteen-year-old farm girl, her summons to the Dauphin to act like a king, her courage in battle, her martyrdom and subsequent rehabilitation and (much later) canonization—all this stuff out of which heroes are fashioned." At the age of nineteen, she was given a chance to gain her freedom by denouncing her purpose. In the play of *Joan of Lorraine*, Maxwell Anderson, wrote describing her purpose:

*"I know this now. Every man gives
his life for what he believes.
Every women gives her life for what
she believes. Sometimes people
believe in little or nothing, and so
they give their lives to little or
nothing. One life is all we have, and
we live it as we believe in living it
and then it's gone. But to surrender
who you are and to live without
belief is more terrible than dying-
Even more terrible than dying young."*

Much like the use of steam, gasoline, electricity, or atomic energy to give power to machinery, vision provides the necessary power to unleash the esprit de corp of the human soul to accomplish mighty things in society. A biblical proverb advises, "Where there is no vision, the people perish." Like all other principles, vision transcends, culture, ethnicity, age, and time. It operates regardless of how one feels about it. Vision is an unchanging law and must precede every result.

Consciously or unconsciously humanity relies on vision to provide the motivation to get things done and achieve goals. The motivation is the power by which people can overcome the adversity and negative influences in life. Inertia is the restraining force that keeps progress from happening and tends to remain in a state of rest or complacency. Rocks lie in the mountainside for thousands of years until there is a force by which they move out of place. Vision serves the same purpose in people. The physical, spiritual, mental, and social human dimensions remain inert until motivating forces set them into motion. Individually and socially, there needs to be the correct vision that is strong enough to produce the appropriate outcomes. What essentially moves people and society forward down the path of life is a deep vision.

What is the purpose of my life?

_____
_____
_____
_____
_____
_____
_____
_____
_____
_____
_____
_____
_____
_____
_____
_____
_____
_____
_____

*The **Small Wonders** of Leadership*
Vision - The Future Must Be Created

Define my personal, relationship, family, community, and professional vision.

_____

_____

_____

_____

_____

_____

_____

_____

_____

_____

_____

_____

_____

_____

_____

_____

_____

_____

_____

_____

_____

_____

The **Small Wonders** of Leadership

Vision - The Future Must Be Created

How will I be remembered?

_____
_____
_____
_____
_____
_____
_____
_____
_____
_____
_____
_____
_____
_____
_____
_____
_____
_____
_____

The **Small Wonders** _of Leadership_
Vision - The Future Must Be Created

ENTHUSIASM & OPTIMISM

Mirror Images Of Strength

The influence of a leader is interpreted in the flow of such attributes as contagious enthusiasm and optimism. To catalogue the importance of the attribute, at least in a preliminary way, is the force that is created when such an attitude is unleashed. The single characteristic and interplay of the mirror images infinitely creates power to infuse the hearts and minds of both the leader and follower. It is one of the most solid and durable traits an individual can possess. Ralph Waldo Emerson said, "Nothing great was ever achieved without enthusiasm."

The most explosive elements in accomplishing great things and those who tend to achieve more in their human existence ignite enthusiasm and optimism. The great strength to crush life's problems and bear the heavy weight lies in the attitude. The encrusted routine of life requires a motivating force to recognize the creativity and hope of humanity.

Sir Edward V. Appleton, the Scottish physicist whose scientific discoveries made worldwide broadcasting possible and won him a Nobel Prize, was asked for the secret of his amazing achievements, "It was enthusiasm." He said, "I rate enthusiasm even above professional skill." At the root of enthusiasm lies the power and freedom to rise above the dark abyss of hardships and challenges to accomplish the goals and remain persistent to the purpose.

Columnist Sydney Harris published insight into well-known people who gave a significant contribution in the midst of their own deficiencies.

> *Sir Walter Scott was a trouble to all his teachers and so was Lord Byron. Thomas Edison, as everyone knows, was considered a dullard in school. Pestalozzi, who later became Italy's foremost educator, was regarded as wild and foolish by his school authorities. Oliver Goldsmith was considered almost an imbecile. The Duke of Wellington failed in many of his classes. Among famous writers, Burns, Balzac, Boccaccio, and Dumas made poor academic records, Flaubert, who went on to become France's most impeccable writer, found it extremely difficult to learn to read. Thomas Aquinas, who had the finest scholastic mind of all Catholic thinkers, was actually dubbed "the dumb ox" at school. Linnaeus and Volta did badly in their studies. Newton was last in his class. Sheridan, the English playwright, wasn't able to stay in one school more than a year.*

The strap that binds these famous individuals to their accomplishments even in the presences of difficulties and trials was that of optimism. When everything seems unrelenting and ominous, even at the hands of the most extenuating circumstances, enthusiasm keeps the human spirit alive to endure the adversity. The extraordinary hope and faith of these individuals are cultivated attitudes of confidence to realize the realm of possibilities.

One of the messages from the lectern of any society is perhaps the full measure of how individuals support one another. It is about providing strength and encouragement from where others currently are to where they need to be. There are countless examples throughout history that sets the social tone of the community. One of the greatest influential leaders of modern times was no other than Winston Churchill. One of the finer qualities, which he possessed, was optimism. In the darkest days of world history, the German regime was quickly defeating Western Europe. History discloses the centrality of contagious enthusiasm. He said, "Do not let us speak of darker days; let us speak rather of stern days. These are not dark days; these are great days—the greatest days our country has ever lived; and must all thank God that we have been allowed, each of us according to our stations, to play a part in making these days memorable in the history of our race." On June 4, as the evacuation of Dunkirk was ending, Churchill spoke to the House of Commons:

> *We shall go on to the end, we shall fight in France, we shall fight on the seas and oceans, we shall fight with growing confidence and growing strength in the air, we shall defend our island, whatever the cost may be, we shall fight on the beaches, we shall fight on the landing grounds, we shall fight in the fields and in the streets, we shall fight in the hills: we shall never surrender, and even if, which I do not for a moment believe, this island or a large part of it were subjugated and starving, then our Empire beyond the seas, armed and guarded by the British fleet, would carry on the struggle, until in, God's good time, the new world, with all its power and might, steps forth to the rescue and the liberation of the old.*

This form of optimism is highly contagious—the kind that moves individuals from everyday insecurities and a victim mentality to a position of responsibility to act on their own. This force comes with acknowledgment of the unlimited potential of knowing one has the ability to think and act beyond the current circumstance. Commander William Robert Anderson who submarined in the Nautilus under the North Pole from the Pacific to the Atlantic Ocean carried a card in his wallet: "I believe I am always divinely guided. I believe I will always take the right road. I believe that God will always make a way, even when there appears to be no way."

Brilliant and influential leaders set the tone for those who reside within their stewardship. They provide the strength to broadly carry the demands that are squarely placed upon them to inspire others. The measure of a great leader is the consistency of communicating to those they lead the message of being present for them, not only in the good times, but also the bad times. Consequently, the clear line between leader and follower is the responsibility to be an optimist and not a pessimist; the duty is incumbent on everyone who expects to live in a harmonious society. The appropriate attitude offers a broadening and deepening foundation from which to effectively govern the social order.

There are no doubts that part of life's journey encounters a troubled world with discord outside the safety of the individual cocoon. Such a foundation brings into the forefront for such mirror images of contagious enthusiasm and optimism. The responsibility of all people is to do and to be. It is the duty of everyone to strive for better days ahead and soften the hardships even in the face of misfortune. Such historical leaders in the vein of George Washington, Thomas Jefferson, and Benjamin Franklin to Franklin D. Roosevelt and Dwight D. Eisenhower showed the way from the United States of America's independence to the battlegrounds of World War II, to walk with heads held high with optimism.

An optimistic and enthusiastic attitude does not require perfection of character rather the ability to rise to the occasion and act upon the opportunities rather than being lost in the maze of perceived insecurities and deficiencies of the victim mentality. The positive mentality is not reserved only for those who sit in the tower of leadership; it rests on the support of personal accountability and responsibility to choose one's own attitude. Those who behave according to the core value are simply honoring the duty of hope.

Many have resigned to the fact that political unrest, warfare, and economic destruction runs rampant throughout the world.

Is there any wonder why there is a basic need for enthusiasm and optimism? There is adequate support in the mirror images that will guide everyone safely through the world's crisis. Irrespective of the dark horizon that will chronically test the will power of all humanity, there must never be a position of giving up hope or harboring the tendency of despair. Paul Fussell, *The Great War and Modern Memory* writes about man-made despair, "A grumpy cynicism pervades politics in so many places on this planet. Holocausts, famine pestilence, and tides of refugees have taken a terrible toll on human hope, with much of that toll coming from man-made, avoidable disasters."

Turning back some of the pages of recent U.S. history is the story of the World Trade Center. Shortly after the attack, Mayor Giuliani became a hero. He inspired hope to all New Yorkers when they needed it most. Nine days after the attack an editorial in the *New York Times* read, "He moves about the stricken city like a God. People want to be in his presence. They want to touch him. They want to praise him. The governor defers to him. The president seems somehow inadequate beside him. He is not only respected, but revered. And not only revered, but loved." The power of influence that Giuliani obtained was in the small wonders of enthusiasm and optimism.

In all of the discussions, optimism is likened to the sun, which lights the paths before us with enthusiasm for the great things that lie ahead and cast the shadows of despair behind which traditionally frostbites individuals to stay in one place. People need to proceed with confidence and determination for meaningful contribution and a fulfilling life. Enthusiasm and optimism permits the human race to "press forward" even in the most trying times of life's journey.

What makes me enthusiastic?

_____

_____

_____

_____

_____

_____

_____

_____

_____

_____

_____

_____

_____

_____

_____

_____

_____

_____

*The **Small Wonders** of Leadership*
Enthusiasm & Optimism - Mirror Images Of Strength

How would I remain optimistic in a difficult situation?

_____
_____
_____
_____
_____
_____
_____
_____
_____
_____
_____
_____
_____
_____
_____
_____
_____
_____
_____

*The **Small Wonders** of Leadership*
Enthusiasm & Optimism - Mirror Images Of Strength

Where do I find strength?

_____

_____

_____

_____

_____

_____

_____

_____

_____

_____

_____

_____

_____

_____

_____

_____

_____

_____

_____

_____

The **Small Wonders** *of Leadership*
Enthusiasm & Optimism - Mirror Images Of Strength

MASTER COMMUNICATOR

Influence People With Honor

In the vast halls of leadership portraits, the framing captures the role of leadership within the best interest of the group. The picture portrays a person who can support the people to the extent in which the group can respond. The essence of the leader is not individual rather an affair of the total group.

To capture the whole person and the varying degrees of personalities and uniqueness, a leader must communicate as a trend towards the needs, wants, shared attitudes, and expectation not only of the social structure, but also of every individual who belongs. As a leader supports the followers, the face of communication must be effective to appropriately direct the group beyond the current environment into a posture of better things to come.

The skill of communication requires an assessment of one's abilities to categorically understand how to activate, rally, guide, inspire, and command to satisfy the masses. The common relationship between leader and follower depends largely on the strap of communication.

The leader becomes central to the success and unity of the group. As told in William F. Whyte's, *Street Corner Society*, the story of the Norton Street boys, a Boston street-corner gang of all different ages primarily in their teens and twenties with an identifiable social order in the group. The leader of the group was Doc; below him were Mike, Danny, and Long John; beneath them were Nusty, Angelo, Frank, and a number of other boys. Danny was the leader inspiring, guiding, activating, and demanding. "In his absence," an observer reported, "the members of the gang are divided into a number of small groups. There is no common activity or general conversation. When the leader appears, the situation changes strikingly. The small units form into one large group. The conversation becomes general, and unified actions frequently follow. The leader becomes the central point in the discussion. A follower starts to say something, pauses when he notices the leader is not listening, and begins again when he has the leader's attention. When the leader leaves the group, unity gives way to the divisions that existed before his appearance."

The group turns on the ability to communicate and more important the leader turns on the ability to effectively communicate. The towering figures of history have been able to broaden the landscape of followership through the power of their message. History has proven the most successful communities and societies were those where the leader had a sharp distinction in communicating.

The ultimate test of such leadership is transforming change and eventually stability. Take the examples of such leaders in the depth of despair, honoring the dead, defining a new day of opportunity, inspiring hope and courage, and setting set standards.

Theodore Roosevelt's speech while serving as a New York assemblyman on January 26, 1883, *Duties of American Citizenship*:

> *Of course, in one sense, the first essential for a man's being a good citizen is his possession of the home virtues of which we think when we call a man by the empathic adjectives of manly. No man can be a good citizen who is not a good husband and a good father, who is not honest in his dealings with other men and women, faithful to his friends and fearless in the presence of his foes, who has not got a sound heart, a sound mind, and a sound body; exactly as no amount of attention to civil duties will save*

a nation if the domestic life is undermined, or there is lack of the rude military virtues which alone can assure a country's position in the world. In the free republic the ideal citizen must be one willing and able to take arms for the defense of the flag, exactly as the ideal citizen must be the father of many healthy children. A race must be strong and vigorous; it must be a race of good fighters and good breeders, else its wisdom will come to naught and its virtue be ineffective; and no sweetness and delicacy, no love for and appreciation of beauty in art or literature, no capacity for building up material prosperity can possibly atone for the lack of the great virile virtues....

In all the enormity of responsibility of a leader, they communicate the set standards for the social group, which they lead. One of the most fundamental tenets of leadership is providing the vision and expectation of the collective attitudes and shared values.

Winton Churchill will be known as one of the most prolific communicators of the 20th century. Of note, Winston Churchill was born with a speech impediment like Demosthenes and others in history. The evacuation of Dunkirk on May 26 where French and British troops were rescued from the imposing forces of the Germans code name "Operation Dynamo" began with 338,000 troops being transported onto thousands of ships while the RAF kept the Luftwaffe occupied. On June 4th, 1940, Churchill delivered his speech to the House of Commons; *We Shall Fight on the Beaches.*

I have, myself, full confidence that if all do their duty, if nothing is neglected, and if the best arrangements are made, as they are being made, we shall prove ourselves once again able to defend our Island home, to ride out the storm of war, and to outlive the menace of tyranny, if necessary for years, if necessary alone. At any rate, that is what we are gong to try to do. That is the resolve of His Majesty's Government-every man of them. That is the will of Parliament and the nation. The British Empire and the French Republic, linked together in their cause and in their need, will defend to the death their native soil, aiding each other like good comrades to the utmost of their strength. Even though large tracts of Europe and many old and famous States have fallen or may fall into the grip of the Gestapo and all the odious apparatus of Nazi rule, we shall not flag or fail.

We shall go on to the end, we shall fight in France, we shall fight on the seas and oceans, we shall fight with growing confidence and growing strength in the air, we shall defend our Island, whatever the cost may be, we shall fight on the beaches, we shall fight on the landing grounds, we shall fight in the fields and in the streets, we shall fight in the hills; we shall never surrender, and even if, which I do not for a moment believe, this Island or a large part of it were subjugated and starving, then our Empire beyond the seas, armed and guarded by the British fleet, would carry on the struggle, until, in God's good time, the New World, with all its power and might, steps forth to the rescue and the liberation of the old.

All of this does not mean leadership is found solely on the one trait of being a great orator, but who else to provide the strength and encouragement than the leader who is confident and intervenes at every level to support, guide, and effectively communicate the goals. It comes down to the concrete ability to deliver the message to commit the followers to the purpose and the ideals.

On July 4th, 1939, Lou Gehrig delivered his *Farewell to Baseball Address* in front of all of his teammates and Yankee fans. After suiting up in a Yankees uniform of 2,130 consecutive games, the 36 year old retired. The amazing aspect of the speech was not to wallow in self-pity, rather to express gratitude to the masses who always supported him. The servant leader principle is self-evident; it's not about the leader as it is about those who follow. Leaders have the ability to effectively communicate in all layers of life.

Of Fans, for the past two weeks you have been reading about a bad brake I got. Yet, today I consider myself the luckiest man on the face of the earth. I have been in ballparks for seventeen years and have never received anything but kindness and encouragement from you fans.

Look at these grand men. Which of you wouldn't consider it the highlight of his career to associate with them for even one day?

Sure, I'm lucky. Who wouldn't consider it an honor to have known Jacob Ruppert—also the builder of baseball's greatest empire, Ed Barrow—to have spent the next nine years with that wonderful little fellow Miller Huggins—then to have spent the next nine years with that outstanding leader, that smart student of psychology—the best manager in baseball today, Joe McCarthy!

Sure, I'm lucky. When the New York Giants, a team you would give your right arm to beat, and vice versa, sends you a gift, that's something! When everybody down to the grounds keepers and those boys in white coats remember you with trophies, that's something.

When you have a wonderful mother-in-law who takes sides with you in squabbles against her own daughter, that's something. When you have a father and mother who works all their lives so that you can have an education and build your body, it's a blessing! When you have a wife who has been a tower of strength and shown more courage that you dreamed existed, that's the finest I know.

So, I close in saying that I might have had a tough break—but I have an awful lot to live for.

Lou Gehrig eventually died from the crippling disease that now bears his name.

One of the greatest traits is the sure and steady quality of communication. The stomach has a voice and it speaks to every language and dialect in the world. Oftentimes, it is clearer than the spoken word. Many individuals can be misinterpreted for various reasons, but there is no misunderstanding when the stomach communicates hunger. The greatest ability in life is to communicate with maximum effectiveness using the tool directly beneath the nose.

Effective communicators can shape not only personal and organizational layers, but also entire nations. In the hundreds of acts of leaders communicating effectively, none other than *"I Have a Dream"* speech imposed heights of inspiration, passion, and motivation. Martin Luther King, a pastor of a Baptist church in Montgomery, Alabama and one of the principle leaders of the United States civil rights movements, made national notoriety when he helped mobilize the black boycott of the Montgomery bus system in 1955. He organized the boycott, after Rosa Parks refused to give up her seat on the bus to a white man. The 382-day boycott led the bus company to change its regulations and the Supreme Court declared such segregation unconstitutional. In August 1963, Martin Luther King led an enormous civil rights march in Washington, D.C. and delivered his famous; "I Have a Dream" speech predicting a day when the promise of freedom and equality for all would become a reality in America.

The I Have a Dream speech pierced the hearts and minds of the American culture touching people's inner aspirations. The message resonated with all those who heard it. On that given day, the masses became something much larger than themselves ultimately stretching the American social fabric. On July 2, President Lyndon B. Johnson had no choice but to sign into law the Civil Rights Act of 1964.

Arguably, a critical part of leadership is the basic qualification to develop and use the skill and power of communication. It is usually the biggest single factor in creating a favorable atmosphere for individuals to reside and commit to the organization.

"Without good communication all effective teamwork is impossible. For how can one perform effectively if he lacks essential information, or if his efforts are not coordinated with others? If any joint enterprise is to be successful, the responsibility and the degree of authority must be spelled out in clear, unmistakable terms. Then not only will the individual to whom responsibility is delegated know the extent of his responsibility and the limits of his authority, but others in the organization will also have a clear understanding of team objectives and team play; otherwise their progress will be retarded."

One of the greatest methods of communication ever developed was in the team concept of the "Huddle." It is a process where every player quickly communicates the objectives, eliminates failures, and increases synergy among everyone. The leader of the group must take the lead in the communication and send the message that everyone is dependent upon each other for the common goal.

Furthermore, communication bridges the gap between diverse groups: different backgrounds, expectations, objectives, and personalities to work harmoniously together. It is central to any organization.

What would I say to inspire
people during a crisis?

_____

_____

_____

_____

_____

_____

_____

_____

_____

_____

_____

_____

_____

_____

_____

_____

_____

_____

_____

_____

_____

*The **Small Wonders** of Leadership*
Master Communicator - Influence People With Honor

What is my style of communication
during various situations?

_____
_____
_____
_____
_____
_____
_____
_____
_____
_____
_____
_____
_____
_____
_____
_____
_____
_____
_____

*The **Small Wonders** of Leadership*
Master Communicator - Influence People With Honor

How do I express the true feeling behind the message?

_____
_____
_____
_____
_____
_____
_____
_____
_____
_____
_____
_____
_____
_____
_____
_____
_____
_____

*The **Small Wonders** of Leadership*
Master Communicator - Influence People With Honor

NO MAN IS AN ISLAND

A Basic Need To Belong To A Community

On August 13, 1863, there was an obscure obituary placed in the *New York Herald* saying, "Philip Nolan, died on board the U.S. Corvette Levant on the 11ᵗʰ of May, 1863, buried at sea, latitude 2 degrees, 11 minutes South longitude 131 degrees West." Based on the brief description most people would not have known the story of Philip Nolan. There are thousands of readers who would have taken note of the obituary had the officer of the "Levant" reported: Philip Nolan died May 11, 1863, THE MAN WITHOUT A COUNTRY. For it was Philip Nolan, who was generally known as THE MAN WITHOUT A COUNTRY.

Philip Nolan served in the United States Army and was deceived by a very crafty person by the name of Aaron Burr who wished to establish a new nation west of the Mississippi river, with himself as emperor. Philip Nolan was found guilty of treason in the court of law. At the close of the trial, the President of the court asked Philip whether he wished to say anything to show that he had always been faithful to the United States, he cried out, in a fit of frenzy, "Damn the United States! I wish I may never hear of the United States again!"

He never did hear of her name again. From that moment, September 23, 1807, till the day he died, May 11, 1863, he never heard of the United States name again. For that half-century and more he was a man without a country.

He was placed on board government vessels and was not

allowed to come within a hundred miles of American territory. He was transferred over 20 times from vessel to vessel. With every transfer, the orders were given to the next vessel that read:

"Sir—You will receive from Lieutenant Neale the person of Philip Nolan, late a lieutenant in the United States Army. This person on his trial by court-martial expressed, with an oath, the wish that he might 'never hear of the United States again.' The Court sentenced him to have his wish fulfilled. For the present, the execution of the order is entrusted by the President to this Department. You will take the prisoner on board your ship, and keep him there with such precautions as shall prevent his escape. You will provide his with such quarters, rations, and clothing as would be proper for an officer of his late rank, if he were a passenger on your vessel on the business of his government. The gentlemen on board will make any arrangements agreeable to themselves regarding his society. He is to be exposed to no indignity of any kind, nor is he ever unnecessarily to be reminded that he is a prisoner. But under no circumstances is he ever to hear of his country or to see any information regarding it; and you will especially caution all the officers under your command to take care, that, in the various indulgences which may be granted, this rule, in which his punishment is involved, shall not be broken.

It is the intention of the Government that he shall never again see the country, which he has disowned. Before the end of your cruise you will receive orders which will give affect to this intention."

Respectfully your,
W. Southard, for the Secretary of the Navy

Nolan was not allowed to talk with the others on the ship unless an officer was present. All information regarding the United States was not permitted for reading or discussion. He chose to wear his army issued uniform but was not allowed to wear the buttons that bore the initials of the country.

At the time of death, a doctor found a slip of paper in the Bible, where Nolan had written his last request. It said: "Bury me in the sea; it has been my home, and I love it. But won't someone set up a stone in my memory at Fort Adams or at Orleans, that my disgrace may not be more than I ought to bear? Say on it,

In Memory of
Philip Nolan
Lieutenant in the Army of the United States,
He loved his country as no other man ever loved:
But no one deserved less at her hands.

May God bless us, that we may forever be loyal to that country to which we also owe our allegiance and our gratitude.

The same tendency prevails for all humanity. There is a basic need to belong to a community to not only be loved, but to love. Unless people draw closer to their fellowmen, there will be tremendous loneliness and emptiness in life. The abundance of life is serving others for a better world. When people concern themselves with others, there is less time to be concerned with themselves. If there is a focus on the simple principles of human of conduct and simple acts of service, the social lines will deteriorate and eventually will have little to no significance. The social identity will not be as important as the identity of every person. Arguably, the standard practice of living life solely for the benefit of self has very little purpose. The dead trees whose branches have withered produce no fruit. One must live to produce fruit, which are a benefit for everyone to enjoy. The more one serves the greater the substance of the person.

Many years ago, Ernest Hemingway wrote a best seller called, *For Whom the Bell Tolls*. The theme of the Spanish Civil War came from the theme of John Donne's poem: "No man is an island entire to itself; every man is a piece of the continent, a part of the main. If a clod be washed away by the sea, Europe is the less…any man's death diminishes me, because I'm involved in mankind." Everybody benefits when other people accomplish great things. When there is a break through in medicine everyone benefits; when someone invents some device all are enriched. It applies in the horizontal areas of education, financial, social, and spiritual. Individuals, like planets, have orbits and it is the attraction of others that holds everyone in place.

In the Declaration of Independence, Thomas Jefferson said, "In the support of this declaration, we mutually pledge to each other our lives, our fortunes and our sacred honor." It is the responsibility of all people to care for one another. What can be said largely about pledging life to each other? It remains only to ask: What is the purpose of life, if it is not to support others and the community? Such harmony exists when the citizens of the society behave in accordance to the set standards or ethics. It is the knot that binds the community together.

Why would individuals reach out to me?

_____
_____
_____
_____
_____
_____
_____
_____
_____
_____
_____
_____
_____
_____
_____
_____

*The **Small Wonders** of Leadership*
No Man Is An Island - A Basic Need To
Belong To A Community

What support do I provide others?

_____
_____
_____
_____
_____
_____
_____
_____
_____
_____
_____
_____
_____
_____
_____
_____
_____

*The **Small Wonders** of Leadership*
No Man Is An Island - A Basic Need To
Belong To A Community

Why does belonging to a community matter?

_____
_____
_____
_____
_____
_____
_____
_____
_____
_____
_____
_____
_____
_____
_____
_____

The **Small Wonders** *of Leadership*
No Man Is An Island - A Basic Need To
Belong To A Community

SMALL WONDERS of INSPIRATION

By James M. Morrison

In order to achieve the future, one must improve the present and before any individual can improve the present, they must first improve their attitude. It is the dominant character trait to grow and achieve the possibilities of life. People's minds can certainly grow and expand, along with the other small wonders of leadership to move from the contracting positions of life to the stretching opportunities to achieve full ambition.

Leadership is about leading people. They inspire and motivate people to help them discover their own ability to accomplish great things. They drive the workforce to achieve vision, strategy and commitment by continuously being attentive to the basic human needs of the labor force.

People are in the exact situation because they are deliberately throwing the joys of life and everything that goes with it out in the garbage because they choose not to work.

When everything seems vulnerable and ominous, even at the hands of the most extenuating circumstances and challenges, it is vision that keeps the human and organizational spirit alive and to bear the adversities.

The doors of influence hinge on central characteristics that form an individual. The most basic swing is the character and competence of the individual, which opens the rights for leadership authority.

The movement of leadership is not built on duplicity, manipulation, exploitation, and false representation rather the vital aspects of momentum through the direct environment of followership.

Emotional maturity is about controlling the instinctive tendency to react rather than letting raw emotions prevail.

Like all other principles, vision transcends culture, ethnicity, age, and time. It operates regardless of how one feels about it. Vision is an unchanging law and must precede every result.

The role or roles a leader plays is determined on the whole character and purpose they design for themselves. The roles will vary tremendously, but never to the degree where they are phony and duplicitous in his or her behavior.

An individual can have the surface signs, of being an example however; they are more related to being empty inside of the true character in personal and professional identity when the role is villain masked as a hero. Overtime, the person who is faking leadership will eventually be exposed and the mask of fraud will be revealed.

Throughout time, individuals gave their lives for their vision and subordinated life to the purpose and cause, to the extent in which it represented their life.

Optimism is likened to the sun, which lights the paths before us with enthusiasm for the great things that lie ahead and cast the shadows of despair behind which traditionally frostbites individuals to stay in one place.

The key and the greatest working capital of any workforce is the knowledge base of employees.

Authentic character is living the values in environments when it is most difficult to stand tall and do what is right.

Anything less than a conscious effort to "A" is a subconscious effort to "B" the subconscious effort to "B" is a declaration of non-support.

Day-by-day, hour-by-hour, one builds the character that will determine their place and standing in their ability to earn the right to have followers.

Leaders must be committed to the most outwardly pronounced character ethics, which is the greatest sustaining power to those they lead.

Leaders are not reliant on others to validate their existence rather they get their sense of value from validating by what lies inside and not from external forces. There is an internal strength for what and who they are. The power is within and not at the exploits of others weaknesses and at the necessity to undermine what others do not have.

Great leaders channel their egotistical needs away from themselves for the best interest of those they serve.

In most cases, it is difficult to share the hard ground truth of reality. It makes most individuals very uncomfortable. Unfortunately, most people confuse parenting and leadership as being a friend, as opposed to being a trusted parent and leader providing feedback and essential counsel.

Leaders must capture the qualities of the expressed values and foundational principles and furthermore become, to a much larger degree, performers to execute on the nature of explicit purpose in which they represent.

The hallmark ambition is to be self-aware in accurately perceiving feelings and emotions of others and to control emotional needs to actively choose appropriately what to say and do.

Despite the importance of the physical needs of food, water and air to sustain the physical body, people have psychological emotional needs of understanding, purpose and contribution. What physical air is to the body, psychological air is to the human soul.

The most influential and consequential type of leader is the individual who protects those they lead.

The sharp view of leadership is the required strict accountability of self and to the extent in which it will provide a much stronger landscape to hold others accountable for their own behavior and performance.

So many leaders are like chameleons; they change their hues to fit the situation, which tends to confuse those they lead. Such change burdens their followers to determine who the leader is and what direction is being pursued.

One of the central points of leadership is straightforward talk.

Eyebrow raising employees can always find a reason why the desires of authority should not and cannot be carried out to the extent in which it drives behaviors of struggle to undermine authority reinforcing their position that authority is wrong. It is from the person in authority that subordinates are trying to break free to demonstrate their own competency in a manipulative style.

The most decisive course of action is simply being the example, lighting the path of those who follow. It is not just about attitude, diligence, or skills of knowing what to do and how to do it rather about performing some of the most inconsequential jobs. If a leader can lead by example and do what is asked of others, their effectiveness and ability to lead will be tremendously enhanced.

Prolonging the inevitable hard conversation will not only compound matters for the employee, but also force other team members to question the leader's strength to resolve conflict and to effectively lead.

The setting off in peoples' minds is thinking a rush to Mercy instead of an appropriate charge to Justice—the thoughts are to protect from offensives and to shy away from correctness, even when it might be helpful.

Most do not like making the critical and most difficult decisions. It is not natural to place oneself at positions of heavy responsibility. The hard decisions rest entirely and squarely upon the shoulders of the leader and it become his or her full responsibility.

The vital power of people is they are not a product of their environment, genetics and psyche, rather they stand-alone and independent from such settings. They have the ability to choose. In truth, there are countless opportunities to spring up to great heights and experience the full chambers of life. The utmost influence of a leader is the power of choice.

The declaration that one might need help and has gaps is a sign of a truly self-aware and trustworthy person rather than turning to the classic means of pushing fault.

The conflict of asking for feedback appears to be an outwardly position of insecurity. However, this theory is on the contrary. The premise is sharply different; the very nature of seeking feedback demonstrates accountability, strength and wisdom.

RESOURCES

Chapter 1 - LEADER & FOLLOWER

P. 1   **"All nations seek:** Quoted in Thomas Jefferson Research Center Bulletin, No 23, December 1967.

P. 2   **"The role of:** James M. Morrison, *The Choice of Leadership: Bridging the Gap Between Simplicity and Complexity* (Salt Lake City, 2011), p. 17.

P. 3   **"The king now:** John Hanning Speke, *Journal of the discovery of the source of the Nile* (New York: Harper & Brothers, 1894), p. 290.

P. 4   **"Conformity does not:** James MacGregor Burns, *Leadership* (New York: Harper & Row Publisher), p. 291.

P. 4   **"A house divided:** Lincoln's remarks from "A House divided," speech, in which he accepted the nomination for U.S. senator at the Republican State Convention in Springfield, Illinois (June 16, 1885)

P. 5   **"He cannot inspire:** David C. McClelland, *Power: The Inner Experience* (New York: Irvington, 1975), p. 260.

P. 5   **"Leadership is not:** Arthur F. Bentley, *The Process of Government* (Chicago: University of Chicago Press, 1908), quoted at p. 223; see ch. 8, passim.

P. 6   **"Suppose a nation:** John Adams, *Works*, Vol. II, pp. 6-7, diary entry for February 22, 1756.

Chapter 2 - CIVILITY

P. 13   **Alfred Adler:** Heinz Ansbacher and Rowena R. Ansbacher, The Individual Psychology of Alfred Adler (New York: Basic Books, 1956), pp. 103-107, 125-129.

P. 16   **Amish school shooting:** David Kocieniewski, "Man Shoots 11, Killing 5 Girls, in Amish School" *The New York Times*, October 3, 2006.

P. 16   **"We arrived in this:** Charles Gibson, "Amish Say They 'Forgive' School Shooter" *ABC News,* October 3, 2006.

P. 17   **Guy de Maupassant:** *The Works of Guy de Maupassant* (Roslyn, New York: Black's Reader Service, n.d.,1965), pp. 34–38. Story Retold

P. 18   **"With Malice toward:** John Bartlett, *Familiar Qutotations* (Boston: Little Brown & Co., 1968), p. 640.

Chapter 3 - LEADING IN FRONT

P. 23   **"For to those who:** Lytton Strachey, *The Biography of Florence Nightingale* (VA: A & D Publishing, 2008), p. 22.

P. 24   **"It would be peculiarly:** "Washington's First Inaugural Address, 1789," in *The Harvard Classics, American Historical Documents* 1000-1904,ed. Charles W. Eliot (New York: P.F. Collier and Sons, 19100, pp. 43:242.

P. 35   **"I respect all men:** Charles H. Malik, "Forum Address" (18 November 1975), *BYU Studies* 16, no. 4 (Summer 1976): 54344.

"Men, I now knew: William Manchester, *Goodbye, Darkness:*

P. 26   *A Memoir of the Pacific War* (Boston: Little, Brown and Company, 1980), p. 391.

P. 26   **"The sharp view:** James M. Morrison, *The Choice of Leadership: Bridging the Gap Between Simplicity and Complexity* (Salt Lake City, Utah, 2011), p. 148.

Chapter 4 - SELF CONTROL

P. 33   **"Some become enslaved:** Richard L. Evans, "Self-Control," *Improvement Era* Dec. 1963, p. 1113.

P. 34   **"A man who:** C.S. Lewis, *Mere Christianity* (New York: Simon & Schuster, 1980), pp, 124-125.

P. 36   **"Underlining one:** James M. Morrison, *The Choice of Leadership: Bridging the Gap Between Simplicity and Complexity* (Salt Lake City, Utah, 2011), p. 88.

P. 37   **"Sometimes we allow:** Sterling W. Sill, *Leadership* (Salt Lake City: Bookcraft, 1960), p. 247.

Chapter 5 - ACCOUNTABILITY

P. 47   **"The leader who:** President N. Eldon Tanner, *Ensign*, November 1975, p. 74.

P. 48   **"The humanitarian theory:** C. S. Lewis, God in the Dock: Essays on Theology and Ethics 1970, p. 294.
Attitude

Chapter 6 - ATTITUDE

P. 53   **While a woman:** This story was shared by a colleague. Another version of the storey was printed in Readers Digest, July 1980. p.21.

P. 54   **"Unfortunately, many:** James M. Morrison, The Choice of Leadership: Bridging the Gap Between Simplicity and Complexity (Salt Lake City: 2011), p. 49.

P. 54   **"The vital power:** James M. Morrison, The Choice of Leadership: Bridging the Gap Between Simplicity and Complexity (Salt Lake City: 2011), p. 123.

P. 55   **"One day Ali Hafed:** Sterling W. Sill, *The Upward Reach* (Salt Lake City: Bookcraft, 1962), pp. 27-30. Story Retold.

Chapter 7 - MUST ACT

P. 63   **"in front of:** Hesiod, *Works and Days, 1.* 287, as cited in John Bartlett, *Familiar Quotations*, 14th ed., (Boston: Little, Brown and Co., 1968), p. 67.

P. 64   **"I will work:** Sterling W. Sill, *Leadership* (Slat Lake City; Bookcraft, 1958), p. 133.

P. 66   **"He was not:** Donald T. Phillips, *Lincoln On Leadership* (New York: Hachett Book Group, 1992), pp. 170-171.

Chapter 8 - VISION

P. 73   **Throughout time:** James M. Morrison, *The Choice of Leadership: Bridging the Gap Between Simplicity and Complexity* (Salt Lake City, Utah, 2011), p. 41.

P. 74   **"What kind of men:** Steven Pressfield, Gates of Fire: An Epic Novel of the Battle of Thermopylae (New York, Bantam Dell, 1999), p. 6.

P. 74   **"When everything seems:** James M. Morrison, *The Choice of Leadership: Bridging the Gap Between Simplicity and Complexity* (Salt Lake City, Utah, 2011), p. 47.

P. 76   **Let every nation know:** John F. Kennedy inaugural address January 20, 1961.

P. 76   **The birth of Joan:** James MacGregor Burns, *Leadership* (New York: Harper & Row Publisher, 1978), p. 242.

P. 77   **I know this now:** Maxwell Anderson, "Joan of Lorraine" New York: Dramatists Play Services, 1946.

P. 77   **Where there is:** Proverbs 29:18, King James.

Chapter 9 - ENTHUSIASM & OPTIMISM

P. 83   **"It was enthusiasm:** Norman Vincent Peale, *Enthusiasm Makes The Difference* (New York: Ballantine Books, 1967), p. 12.

P. 84   **Sir Walter Scott:** *Deseret News*, 20 October 1960.

P. 85   **"Do not let:** Winston S. Churchill, *These Are Great Days: His Complete Speeches*, ed. Robert Rhodes James (New York: Chelsea House Publishers, 1974), 6;6500.

P. 85   **"I believe I am:** Gordon B. Hinckley, Standing for Something (New York: Three Rivers Press, 2000), p. 129.

P. 87   **"A grumpy cynicism:** Paul Fussell, *The Great War and Modern Memory* (London: Oxford University Press, 1975), p.74.

P. 87   **"He moves about:** Bob Herbert "Cometh the hour, cometh the mayor", *New York Times*, September 21 2001.

Chapter 10 - MASTER COMMUNICATOR

P. 93   **Norton Street boys:** William F. Whyte's, *Street Corner Society* (Illinois: The University of Chicago Press, 1993), p. 3.

P. 94   **"In his absence:** James MacGregor Burns, *Leadership* (New York: Harper & Row Publisher, 1978), p. 289.

P. 94   *Of course:* Theodore Roosevelt's speech while serving as a New York assemblyman, *Duties of American Citizenship,* January 26, 1883.

P. 95   *I have, myself:* Churchill delivered his speech to the House of Commons, *We Shall Fight on the Beaches,* June 4, 1940.

P. 98   **"I Have a Dream:** James M. Morrison, *The Choice of Leadership: Bridging the Gap Between Simplicity and Complexity* (Salt Lake City, 2010), p. 54. Story Retold.

P. 99   **"Without good communication:** Sterling W. Sill, *Leadership,* (Salt Lake City, Bookcraft 1958), p. 208.

Chapter 11 - NO MAN IS AN ISLAND

P. 105   **Philip Nolan, died:** Edward Everett Hale, *The Man Without a Country* (Teddington, Middlesex: Echo-Library, 1863), p. 6.

www.ingramcontent.com/pod-product-compliance
Lightning Source LLC
Chambersburg PA
CBHW031402180326
41458CB00043B/6575/J